Copyright © 2026 Stand Again

All rights reserved.

No part of this publication may be reproduced, stored in a retrieval system, or transmitted in any form or by any means - electronic, mechanical, photocopying, recording, or otherwise - without prior written permission from the author, except for brief quotations used in reviews or critical articles.

Stand Again is a registered business operating under ABN 75 563 353 277.

www.standagain.com.au

Disclaimer

This guide is based on lived experience, research, and insights drawn from recovery work with survivors of abuse. It is intended for educational and self-reflective purposes only. It is not a substitute for professional mental health care, diagnosis, or treatment.

Some of the topics discussed may bring up strong emotions or memories. If you feel overwhelmed at any point, pause your reading and consider reaching out to a trusted friend, counsellor, or helpline. You are the best judge of your own readiness and pace.

Any strategies, exercises, or examples included here are suggestions, not prescriptions. Every survivor's healing journey is unique - what works for one person may not work for another. Take what serves you, adapt it to your needs, and leave the rest.

If you are currently in danger or experiencing distress, please seek immediate support from a qualified professional or crisis service in your area.

Copyright © 2026 Stand Again
www.standagain.com.au
Version 2: 17th January 2026

Table of Contents

Introduction 4

The Healthy Emotional Processing Cycle 6

    The Healthy Way 8

How Abuse Hijacks Healthy Emotional Processing 14

    Protective Interrupts 17

        1. Self-Suppression 18

        2. Crisis Shelving 20

        3. Escalation Risk → Survival Switch 22

        4. Dissociative Bypass 24

        Final Thoughts on Protective Interrupts 26

    Abuser-Driven Hijacks 27

        5. Flooding / Overwhelm 28

        6. Misattribution & Meaning-Rewrite 30

        7. Window-Of-Tolerance Conditioning 31

        8. Cue → Response Conditioning 33

        Final Thoughts On Abuser-Driven Hijacks 34

    What Happens if This Remains Broken 37

        1. Emotional Dysregulation 37

        2. Emotional Dissociation 38

        3. Mood Lability 39

Repairing The Emotional Processing Cycle 41

    What To Expect During Repair 43

        When To Get Professional Support 44

    How To Recondition Emotional Processing 45

Stand Again
Support for male victims
of family violence

Step-By-Step Reconditioning 46
Step 1 - Awareness Without Action 49
Step 2 - Controlled Micro-Interrupts 54
Step 3 – Choosing Healthy Alternatives 58
Step 4 - Repetition and Reinforcement 66
Step 5 – Integration And Expansion 71

Conclusion 75
Glossary 76

Introduction

When you come out of an abusive relationship, one of the first things you notice - if you slow down long enough to see it - is that your emotions feel off.

Sometimes they're too big for the situation you're in. Sometimes they're absent altogether. And sometimes, they appear hours or days after the moment that should have sparked them.

It's not because you're "too sensitive." It's not because you're "cold" or "shut down." It's because abuse changes the way you experience and process emotion at a deep level.

Every human being is born with an emotional processing cycle - a natural sequence that helps us understand, express, and learn from what we feel. It's as fundamental to our wellbeing as breathing. We don't think about it; it just happens. In safe environments, this cycle develops freely, giving us the ability to connect to ourselves and to others in an honest, balanced way.

But in abuse, that cycle is deliberately interfered with. Not by accident, not because of "communication issues," but because interrupting your natural emotional process makes you easier to control. In time, that interruption becomes a habit - a survival mechanism - that you start to use automatically, even when the danger has passed.

That's why so many survivors describe feeling disconnected from themselves. Why joy feels muted, sadness feels dangerous, and anger feels uncontrollable. The problem isn't that you "don't know how to feel." It's that the very system you use to process those feelings has been rewired to protect you in an unsafe environment - at the cost of your authenticity.

That's why we don't jump straight into "fixing." Before you can rebuild, you need to see the structure clearly. You need to understand what

Stand Again
Support for male victims
of family violence

healthy emotional processing looks like, how abuse hijacks it, and what living with broken or distorted wiring does to you.

Without this map, attempts at repair can feel confusing, overwhelming, or even reinforce the wrong patterns.

This book will guide you through both parts of the work:

- First, recognising the cycle itself and how it has been damaged.
- Then, step by step, learning how to retrain it back into a healthy rhythm.

Because restoring this processing cycle is more than "feeling better." It's about reclaiming one of the most important parts of yourself: your ability to feel safe in your own emotions.

Before we begin, one reminder: the steps in this book describe common patterns and proven ways to repair them. But recovery is not mechanical — it is deeply human. Your emotions are not just "wires" to be fixed; they are signals of truth, unique to you. What you'll find here is a map. The exact terrain of your healing will still be yours, and your feelings remain the most important guide as you walk it.

The Healthy Emotional Processing Cycle

Healthy Emotional Processing Cycle
How we process and integrate emotional experiences

Step 1: Something Happens

Every emotion begins with a spark. Not everything creates one - only what carries meaning for you comes to the foreground.

It may be **external** (a smile, cancelled plans, a sound, a smell) or **internal** (a thought, a memory, hunger, fatigue).

Step 2: It Sparks an Emotion

The spark activates an immediate emotional signal - happiness, disappointment, anxiety, anger, relief.

At this stage, the feeling is raw and unfiltered: your body's first, honest response.

Step 3: Memory Recall & Conditioning

Your brain instantly searches for similar past experiences. Prior lessons and reinforcement shape how you respond now.

In healthy processing, this builds balance and confidence.

Step 4: Internal Sensation & External Expression

What you feel inside and what you show outside move in sync.

- **Internal sensations** (butterflies, heaviness, warmth, dread)
- **Outward expression** (smiling, crying, frowning).

Each influences the other, creating emotional authenticity.

Step 5: Sense-Making

The raw feeling becomes clear enough to name: *"I feel sad." "I feel angry." "I feel proud."*

This step is about clarity — recognising the emotion itself, without yet explaining it.

Step 6: Learning

From that clarity, you link the feeling to meaning. Lessons are clear, proportionate, and grounded in the situation.

"I feel sad because..."

Trusted voices you invite into your life can help shape this understanding.

Step 7: Storing

Your brain integrates the full sequence — spark, emotion, sensations, expression, meaning, lesson. Each stored memory conditions future responses, reinforcing or refining how you'll process emotions next time.

Memory Storing for Later Recall

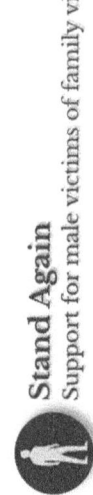

Stand Again
Support for male victims of family violence

Copyright © 2026 Stand Again

The Healthy Way

Every human is born with a built-in process for experiencing emotions.

Some parts happen automatically - before you've even had a chance to think - and others can be shaped by awareness and practice. In healthy environments, this cycle runs freely from start to finish, giving you a complete emotional experience and helping you store it as part of your personal history.

Here's what that process looks like when it's working well:

Step 1. Awareness (External or Internal)

You notice something that matters to you.

Every emotion begins with a spark - an event that sets the process in motion. But not everything in your world creates a spark. Most of what you see, hear, and experience fades into the background – filtered out by the mind. Only certain moments come to the foreground, and those are the ones that hold meaning for you.

That spark can come from the outside world: someone smiling at you, a friend cancelling plans, a sound, a smell, or a change in your environment. Or it can come from within: a passing thought, a sudden memory, or a physical shift in your body like hunger or fatigue.

What matters is not the event itself, but whether it resonates with you. A patch of asphalt might mean nothing to most people, yet for someone who grew up playing street basketball, it can carry a surge of memory and feeling. The sound of construction equipment might be irritating to one person, while for someone who worked construction their whole life, it can feel like home.

Some sparks are almost universal - like the cry of a baby or the warmth of laughter - while others are deeply personal and unique to your history. Either way, the spark is the signal that says: *"This matters. Pay*

Stand Again
Support for male victims
of family violence

attention." It is the first step in transforming raw experience into emotion.

Step 2. Activation

**ced*Your body sparks the first raw feeling.*

When something meaningful catches your attention, your brain and body respond almost instantly. In a fraction of a second, an emotional signal is activated - before you've even had the chance to think it through.

At this stage, the emotion is raw and unfiltered. It's your body's first, honest response to the spark. You might feel a lift of happiness, a drop of disappointment, a jolt of anxiety, a rush of anger, or a wave of relief. Whatever arises in that moment is your system's way of saying: *"This matters."*

Emotions at this stage are less about explanation and more about activation. They are quick, biological signals - changes in your chemistry, heartbeat, and attention - that alert you to the significance of what just happened. They point your awareness toward the event and prepare you to respond.

In healthy processing, this immediacy is not something to control or suppress. It's the necessary starting point - the body's way of flagging meaning and setting the stage for the rest of the cycle.

Step 3. Memory Recall & Conditioning

Your brain checks past experiences to guide your response.

Now, your brain instantly searches your memory for similar events. If you've experienced something like this before, your brain draws on those stored experiences to guide your reaction.
This is also where conditioning plays a role. Positive reinforcement from past experiences helps shape the way you respond today. For example, if your father told you how proud he was when you won a sports game, that memory strengthens feelings of pride and motivation in similar moments.

Even when the recall isn't a perfect match, your brain uses these past emotional lessons as a reference point, helping you interpret the present more quickly and respond in ways that feel grounded and appropriate. In healthy environments, this process builds emotional confidence, because your history of responses guides you toward balance and clarity.

Step 4. Internal Sensation & External Expression

What you feel inside shows up on the outside - and back again.

This is the centre of the emotional experience - where what you feel inside synchronises with how you express it outside.

It's *in sync* and *bidirectional*. Internal sensations and external expressions happen almost simultaneously, each shaping and reinforcing the other.

- **Internal sensations** are the felt experiences inside the body - butterflies in the stomach, a heavy weight in the chest, a rising warmth, or a sense of dread. These are how your body "speaks" emotion to you directly.
- **External expressions** are the outward signals - smiling, frowning, crying, laughing, trembling hands, clenched shoulders, or changes in voice and posture.

These two layers are synchronised and bidirectional. What you feel inside shows up outside almost instantly, and what you do outside can shift how you feel inside. A hug can soften loneliness, a child's laughter can brighten your mood, and even a deep sigh can release tension.

Within this synchrony, there is also space for regulation. You can notice what's happening and guide how much of it you express. Maybe you breathe before speaking, or choose to soften your tone even while angry. Other times, it means shelving the full expression of your feelings until the moment is safe. This isn't denial. The emotion is still real and still present. But you deliberately decide to let the full expression come later, when it won't interfere with your immediate ability to cope or protect. Emergency workers often rely on this to stay focused in crisis, and parents sometimes do the same when they need to protect their children first and process their feelings second.

In healthy environments, this flow feels natural and aligned. Your sensations, your expressions, and your choices work together (even if you may delay it sometimes) - creating emotional authenticity, where what you feel and what you show remain congruent.

Step 5. Sense-Making

You name the feeling for what it is.

This is the shift from *feeling* to *knowing what you feel*.

After the emotion has moved through your body and expression, your mind begins to organise it into something you can recognise. Sense-making isn't about explaining why the feeling arose - it's about naming it clearly for what it is.

"I feel angry." "I feel sad." "I feel proud."

Sometimes you put the words to it deliberately. Other times your brain does the organising automatically, sorting the signals into a coherent emotional picture. Either way, this step gives your experience definition - turning raw sensation into recognised emotion.

Step 6. Learning

You understand what the feeling is teaching you.

From naming the feeling, your mind naturally begins to link it to meaning. This is where you understand *why* the emotion arose and what it can teach you.

In healthy processing, the lesson is clear, proportionate, and grounded in the situation at hand. The scale of your takeaway matches the scale of the event - no more, no less. You don't walk away with an exaggerated story, and you don't miss the real message.

This meaning-making doesn't happen in isolation. The voices you invite into your life - friends, family, mentors, even the media you consume -

can shape how you interpret your feelings. In healthy environments, those influences help you see clearly, reinforcing accurate lessons and offering perspective. The key is trust: giving this interpretive power only to sources you believe act in your best interest.

Through this process, the lessons you take can be subtle or profound. You may come to realise that time with a particular friend leaves you energised. You may notice that a boundary matters to you. Or you may recognise that being tired left you less patient, reminding you of the need for rest.

Each lesson, whether small or life-shaping, is integrated into your understanding of yourself and your world. It's how emotions become not just feelings to move through, but signals that guide your growth.

Step 7. Storing

Your brain files it away, shaping how you'll respond next time.

The final stage of the cycle is storage - where the entire experience is integrated into memory. What gets stored isn't just the event. It's the full package: the spark, the emotion, the sensations, the expression, the meaning, and the lesson.

This step is vital because it shapes how your brain will respond the next time. Each stored memory becomes part of the library your mind searches in Step 3. If your understanding of the emotion was clear and the lesson accurate, that memory strengthens your ability to respond with balance and confidence in the future.

Storage also allows for correction. If you misinterpreted a lesson in the past, a healthier experience can refine or even overwrite it, teaching your brain a more accurate pattern. And through repetition, healthy lessons are reinforced and locked in - becoming trusted guides for future situations.

What's stored is not shaped by you alone. The voices around you - friends, family, culture, even media - can all reinforce which lessons are emphasised, remembered, or repeated. These echoes become part of the memory itself, influencing how strongly it is recalled.

In this way, storing is not passive. It is active conditioning. Every memory you file - both through your own understanding and through the reinforcement of those you trust or allow influence - shapes how your emotions will rise, guide, and resolve the next time life sparks them. It's the bridge between today's experience and tomorrow's emotional intelligence.

Final Thoughts

When this cycle is intact, emotions move the way they're meant to. You feel them, express them, make sense of them, learn from them, and store them for the future. Each time the cycle completes, it strengthens your capacity to process the next one with greater clarity and ease.

In safe relationships and environments, this happens seamlessly - hundreds of times a day, often without you even noticing. A smile, a laugh, a moment of irritation, a flicker of sadness - each completes its course and quietly reinforces your ability to trust yourself.

With that repetition it becomes a foundation: for self-trust, for emotional balance, and for healthy connection with others. It's what allows you to stand in your own experience with confidence, and to meet the world with authenticity.

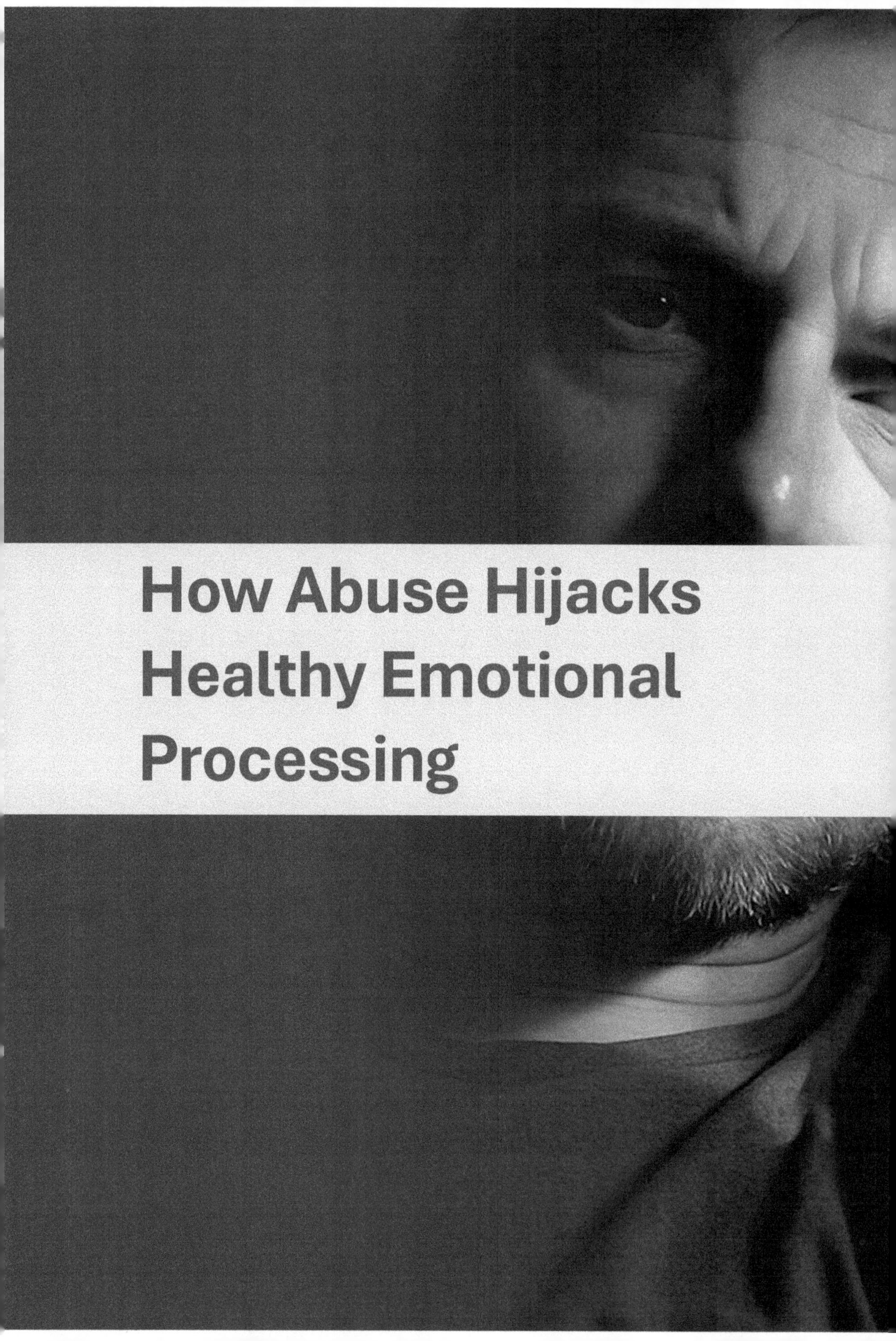

How Abuse Hijacks Healthy Emotional Processing

8 Types of Emotional Abuse Interrupts

How we, or an abuser, can interrupt a healthy emotional processing cycle.

Protective Interrupts
(Survival adaptations you do)

1. Self-Suppression
You shut down the emotion before it's expressed.
- Breaks the sync between internal sensation and external expression at Step 4, leaving the emotion unexpressed and unresolved.

2. Crisis Shelving
You pause the feeling to handle an immediate threat.
- Interrupts the link between sense-making and learning at Steps 5–6, preventing the lesson from being stored and the cycle from completing.

3. Escalation Risk → Survival Switch
Emotion diverts into fawn/flight/fight/freeze.
- Short-circuits the shift from expression to constructive sense-making at Steps 4–5, locking the cycle in survival mode rather than resolution.

4. Dissociative Bypass
You detach completely, skipping the feeling stage.
- Cuts the feedback loop between internal sensation and external expression at Step 4, leaving the emotion disconnected from the body.

Abuser-Driven Hijacks
(What they do to your processing cycle)

5. Flooding / Overwhelm
They swamp you with input faster than you can process.
- Overloads the entire sequence from Steps 2–5, making it impossible to stay present long enough to process or resolve the feeling.

6. Misattribution & Meaning Rewrite
They tell you your feeling is wrong or invalid.
- Overwrites the connection between sense-making and learning at Step 5, replacing your original meaning with one that serves someone else's narrative

7. Conditioning #1 – Window Stretching
They slowly raise the bar for what you'll tolerate.
- Distorts the memory recall filter in Step 3, so current events are compared against a warped baseline rather than a healthy one.

8. Conditioning #2 – Cue → Response Training
They pair a harmless cue with a trained emotional reaction.
- Bypasses healthy evaluation at Step 3, sending you straight into a pre-programmed reaction instead of a fresh emotional appraisal.

Stand Again
Support for male victims of family violence

Copyright © 2026 Stand Again

Abuse doesn't just disrupt the emotional cycle - it hijacks it.

And it does so with precision.

Every time an abuser uses a tactic that sparks an emotional reaction in you, it doesn't just cause pain in the moment. It conditions your mind and body to process that emotion differently the next time.

This isn't a single event. It's repetition over time. The tactics are rehearsed. The triggers become familiar. The impacts compound. And slowly, the natural wiring you were born with - the one that allowed you to experience and process emotions freely - is replaced with something entirely different.

To help make sense of this, we break the cycle into two categories:

- **Protective interrupts** - the emergency brakes you pull on yourself to survive.
- **Abuser-driven hijacks** - the intrusions they use to rewire your system from the outside.

In lived experience, though, these aren't neat boxes. They overlap. They collide. You might suppress your own reaction at the same time the abuser is gaslighting you. You might dissociate while also being flooded. The division here is to help you see the moving parts - but in the moment, it often feels messy, chaotic, and indistinguishable.

And yet, beneath that mess, there is a pattern. The hijacked cycle isn't random. It's survival-driven, designed to protect you under threat, but it comes at a cost:

- Sometimes you shut down your emotions before they even surface, because you've learned that showing them will make things worse.
- Sometimes the abuser interferes directly, twisting the meaning of what you feel so your own memories can't be trusted.
- Sometimes your body is trained to react automatically to certain cues - even ones the abuser can later deny were intentional.

In time, you end up living with an emotional processing cycle that is no longer truly yours. It's been reshaped into a survival version, governed by fear and control. The first step toward reclaiming it is recognising how that hijack happens.

Protective Interrupts

Survival Adaptations You Do

When you're living in an abusive environment, your nervous system learns to prioritise one thing above all else: survival.

That doesn't always mean physical survival - though sometimes it does. It often means emotional survival: getting through the day without further damage, conflict, or exhaustion.

When you are in this environment, you develop what I call ***protective interrupts*** - deliberate or semi-automatic ways of breaking your own emotional processing cycle before it can run its natural course.

These aren't weaknesses. They're survival adaptations to a traumatic experience. Strategies your mind and body create to keep you safe when emotions have become dangerous currency.

In a healthy emotional cycle, you'd feel, express, understand, and learn. But in abuse, if sadness brings ridicule or anger sparks escalation, you learn to cut the process short. You shut it down before the emotion can complete - like pulling the plug on a machine before it finishes its sequence.

Sometimes it's conscious: a decision to "box" your feelings until you're alone. Other times it's automatic: a reflex that kicks in before you've even realised an emotion has begun. Either way, the goal is the same - avoid making the situation worse, even if it means sacrificing your own truth in the moment.

It's important to understand that these interrupts are *not the same as healthy regulation*.

- **Healthy regulation** happens *within* the cycle. You remain with the authentic emotion - anger is still anger, sadness is still sadness - but you guide its expression. You might soften your tone, pause to breathe, or wait for the right context. The cycle still runs, and your expression stays congruent with what you feel inside.
- **Protective interrupts** break the cycle itself. They don't just guide expression - they replace it. You swap the authentic response for one that feels safer in your environment. You're hurt but you smile. You're angry but you go quiet. You're frightened but you perform calmness. The original emotion is buried, and authenticity is disturbed.

Protective interrupts look different for everyone, but they share a single purpose: reducing perceived risk of harm. That might mean shutting down completely, shelving emotions until the "crisis" passes, or shifting instantly into fight, flight, freeze, or fawn. These adaptations come from a deep, instinctive place - your body's way of keeping you alive in an environment that punishes emotional honesty.

1. Self-Suppression

"I Shut It Down"

Self-suppression is the most instinctive and immediate adaptation you develop in an abusive environment. It's the act of recognising the spark of an emotion - anger, sadness, fear, even joy - and cutting it off before it has the chance to take shape. You don't start life doing this. You learn it through repeated punishment, dismissal, or exploitation of your emotions.

In the healthy emotional cycle, the spark flows naturally into sensation and expression. You feel something, and your body reflects it without conscious effort. Self-suppression interrupts that bridge. You clamp down, force a neutral expression, swallow words, and hide the physical cues. Sometimes you even replace them with something safer - a smile, a shrug, a flat tone. Anything that won't trigger the reaction you fear.

The skill develops in microseconds. A facial muscle begins to tighten, or a sigh starts to escape, and you override it. You stop letting cues even begin. Instead, you compress the feeling into an invisible internal pressure.

This is where the **balloon effect** comes in. Each time you suppress, it's like forcing air into a balloon. The emotion doesn't disappear - it's pushed down, filling space inside you. Each time this happens the balloon stretches tighter, pressing against the walls of your emotional self. You can feel it there, squeaking at the edges. That squeak shows up as background anxiety, irritability, or sensitivity - like an irritant rubbing at you from the inside. You hold it as long as you can, but eventually the balloon will either leak, burst suddenly, or release in the wrong direction.

In the short term, self-suppression works. It keeps you safe by preventing escalation. But it carries a heavy cost. Each time you suppress, you block your nervous system from completing the cycle of feeling, expressing, and releasing. You never get to stand down. Even in safe moments, you remain braced, waiting for the next strike.

The danger is that suppression can masquerade as control. You tell yourself you're "keeping the peace" or "holding it together," but really you're living in a constant state of vigilance. Eventually, your authentic inner life and your outer display drift apart. You begin to lose track of which one is really you.

The Process Of Self-Suppression:

- Step 1–2 (Awareness → Activation): A spark of emotion arises - tight chest, shift in breathing, or muscle tension.
- Step 3 (Memory Recall & Conditioning): Past experiences instantly remind you that showing this emotion could escalate danger, ridicule, or punishment.
- Step 4 (Internal Sensation & External Expression): Instead of letting the feeling show naturally, the override command kicks in. You clamp down and either blank your expression or replace it with a "safe" signal (smile, shrug, neutral tone).

- Containment (between Step 4 & 5): The authentic emotion is trapped inside, building invisible pressure - the "balloon effect." The sensation remains but is denied outward release.
- Steps 5-6 (Sense-Making → Learning): Because the emotion never fully surfaces, your sense-making and learning are distorted. What gets reinforced is the lesson that suppression is "safer" than authenticity.
- Step 7 (Storing): The cycle stores suppression itself as the patterned response. In time, this becomes automatic - future sparks trigger suppression before you're even aware of it.

The risk here is that suppression never eliminates the emotion. The "balloon" eventually bursts - sometimes misdirected at the abuser in an explosive moment, other times leaking out onto safe targets who had nothing to do with the cause. Either way, the irregular release compounds shame, reinforces self-doubt, and further distorts your relationship with authentic emotion.

2. Crisis Shelving

"I'll Deal With This Later"

Crisis shelving is what happens when an emotion sparks and begins to move through you, but before it can complete — before you've made sense of it, learned from it, or stored it properly — you deliberately set it aside because something more urgent demands your attention.

In healthy environments, this can be adaptive. A parent who receives devastating news but needs to get their child to safety first. A first responder who feels fear but must act now and process later. The emotion isn't denied — it's consciously paused, with the genuine intention to return to it when the crisis passes.

In abuse, crisis shelving becomes something else entirely.

The abusive environment produces crisis after crisis. There is always another fire to put out, another accusation to manage, another explosion to navigate. The "later" you promised yourself never arrives.

One shelf fills, then another, then another. What began as a temporary pause becomes permanent storage — emotions stacked in a warehouse you never revisit.

The difference between crisis shelving and suppression is where the interruption happens. Suppression stops the emotion before it can be expressed — you clamp down at Step 4, blocking the feeling from ever reaching the surface. Crisis shelving lets the emotion rise, sometimes even partially express — but then it cuts the circuit before Steps 5 and 6 can complete. You feel it. You might even show it briefly. But you don't make sense of it. You don't learn from it. And it never gets properly stored.

This matters because incomplete cycles don't disappear. They accumulate. Each shelved emotion sits unresolved, taking up space in your nervous system. Over time, the shelves groan under the weight. You may not consciously remember what you've stored there, but your body does. It shows up as background tension, chronic fatigue, or a vague sense that something is always unfinished.

The deeper danger is that crisis shelving trains you to believe your emotions are always lower priority than the emergency in front of you. In abuse, that belief is reinforced constantly — your feelings don't matter, the abuser's crisis does. Eventually, you stop even noticing when you're shelving. It becomes automatic. The pause that was meant to be temporary becomes a permanent feature of how you process (or fail to process) emotion.

The Process Of Crisis Shelving:

- Step 1–2 (Awareness → Activation): A spark occurs. The emotion begins to rise.
- Step 3 (Memory Recall & Conditioning): Past experience tells you this feeling is valid — but also that now is not the time.
- Step 4 (Internal Sensation & External Expression): The feeling is felt, sometimes partially expressed. You register it as real.

- Interruption (between Step 4 & 5): A new crisis demands attention. You make the call: "Not now. Later." The emotion is placed on the shelf.
- Steps 5–6 (Sense-Making → Learning): These never occur. The emotion was real, but its meaning is never examined. No lesson is drawn.
- Step 7 (Storing): The experience is stored as incomplete — not resolved, not integrated, just... waiting.

The risk is that shelved emotions don't stay quiet. They leak. They surface at unexpected moments — a disproportionate reaction to something small, a wave of sadness with no obvious cause, a flash of anger years after the event. Or they compound into a generalised heaviness, a sense that you're carrying something you can't name.

Recovery means learning to return to the shelf. Not all at once — that would be overwhelming. But deliberately, with safety, creating space to finally complete the cycles that were interrupted. The emotion that was set aside can still be felt, understood, and released. It's been waiting for you to come back.

3. Escalation Risk → Survival Switch

"I Fawn/Flight/Fight/Freeze"

There are moments in an abusive relationship where an emotion sparks - anger, hurt, frustration, sadness - but before it even has the chance to fully form, something inside you pulls the emergency lever. It's not the same as a deliberate self-suppression, where you decide to bury the feeling to keep the peace. This is different. This is the point where your nervous system believes there is real danger, and it overrides everything else to get you to safety - or at least, to reduce the harm that's coming.

In the healthy emotional processing cycle, a spark of emotion would normally lead you into internal sensation and external expression. You might feel your anger in your chest and voice it, or notice sadness in your body and show it with tears. You would then make sense of it, learn from it, and store the experience in a way that supports future self-trust. But here, the process diverts. The brain doesn't allow you to reach those later steps. Instead, the spark itself becomes a warning - if you show this, it will make things worse.

And so, the survival switch flips. You drop into one of the four instinctive modes:

- **Fawn** - You soften your tone, make yourself agreeable, over-apologise, or try to please in order to de-escalate their anger.
- **Flight** - You physically remove yourself or disengage mentally, trying to get away from the confrontation.
- **Fight** - You meet the escalation with your own pushback, not necessarily because you want to fight, but because your system believes pre-emptive strength might contain or stop the threat.
- **Freeze** - You go still and silent, almost dissociating, in the hope that becoming as non-threatening as possible will make the danger pass.

What's critical to understand is that this survival switch isn't a flaw. It's not a weakness, a lack of willpower, or a sign that you're "overly sensitive." It's the body's emergency protocol kicking in after repeated exposure to high-risk moments. You didn't wake up one day and choose to override your emotional processing cycle. The abuse taught your nervous system that certain expressions or sensations are dangerous.

And at first, these reactions serve their purpose. They reduce the risk of escalation, at least in the moment. But the real danger comes later. Each time the switch is pulled, your body doesn't just log the survival reaction as a temporary detour. It begins to treat it as the *correct outcome*. Instead of storing authentic anger, sadness, or fear, your nervous system files away the fawn, flight, fight, or freeze response as the "right" way to deal with similar events in the future.

This is how the emotional cycle becomes hijacked. You don't just avoid authentic expression in the moment - you train yourself that authentic expression itself is unsafe. You come to believe that the only safe way

to respond is through an *inauthentic survival script*. Anger is replaced with appeasement. Sadness is replaced with silence. Hurt is replaced with withdrawal. The survival response becomes your emotional language.

How Escalation Risk Interrupts The Cycle:

- Step 1–2 (Event → Emotional Spark): An event occurs that would naturally lead to an emotional response.
- Step 3 (Memory Recall / Conditioning): Past experiences remind you what happened last time - and the "safe" response your body stored wasn't authentic expression, but a survival mode.
- Step 4 (Internal Sensation & External Expression): Instead of flowing into healthy expression, the system predicts danger and diverts into fawn, flight, fight, or freeze.
- Steps 5–7 (Sense-Making → Learning → Storing): These are rewritten so that survival mode is stored as the "correct" outcome, locking the pattern in place.
- Next time a similar trigger happens, step 3 retrieves this survival-scripted version - further reinforcing it.

Recovery means retraining the system. At first, this is deliberate and difficult - catching yourself in survival mode and allowing space for the authentic emotion underneath. With safe repetition, your nervous system learns again that authentic expression will not be punished. Slowly, the original cycle - the one you were born with - begins to re-emerge.

4. Dissociative Bypass

"I'm Not Here Anymore"

Dissociative bypass is a survival adaptation where your mind ejects from the emotional cycle entirely. Instead of feeling the spark rise and then deciding whether to express or suppress it, you disconnect from the experience altogether. One moment you are present, the next you feel detached - as if you're watching yourself from the outside, or moving through the scene on autopilot.

This is not the same as freezing. In a freeze response, your body locks while your mind remains hyper-aware, flooded with sensation and racing thought. In dissociation, the opposite occurs: sensation itself becomes muted, distant, or dulled, as though the volume has been turned down on both body and mind. The threat is still happening, but you are no longer fully there to experience it.

In rare, healthy contexts, short-term dissociation can help a person survive extremes - soldiers in combat, first responders in catastrophic events, victims of sudden trauma. But in abuse, it becomes a repeated and involuntary reflex. Your nervous system learns to leapfrog over the middle of the emotional cycle - sensation, expression, sense-making - and drop straight into a numbed state where reality feels blurred and far away.

The cost is profound. Because the emotion was never felt in the first place, there is nothing left "waiting" to be processed later. The event gets stored as a fragmented, low-colour memory, stripped of the emotional context that makes it meaningful. The body may still carry the imprint - tight muscles, digestive pain, chronic fatigue - but the mind has no accessible way to link those symptoms back to the moment. Over time, this can create whole stretches of memory that feel ghostlike: you know they happened, but you can't inhabit them.

The deeper danger is that dissociation trains you to believe absence is safer than authenticity. Instead of learning to regulate emotion, you learn to erase it. That erasure comes with a heavy toll: reduced self-trust, weakened connection to others, and a fractured sense of your own lived story.

How Dissociative Bypass Develops As A Process:

- Step 1–2 (Awareness → Activation): A trigger sparks the beginning of an emotion, but almost immediately the system detects it as overwhelming or unsafe.
- Step 3 (Memory Recall & Conditioning): Instead of drawing on useful past experiences, the system judges this as *beyond*

capacity - signalling that normal processing will not keep you safe.
- Step 4 (Internal Sensation & External Expression): Before sensations and expressions can connect, the "ejection command" fires. The mind detaches, awareness narrows, and sensations dull.
- Steps 5-6 (Sense-Making → Learning): These steps never occur, because the emotion was never fully felt or expressed. Nothing is named, understood, or integrated.
- Step 7 (Storing): The event is stored in fragments - a kind of memory without emotional colour. Recall feels blurry, incomplete, or detached from meaning.

Recovery from dissociation requires a different path than suppression or survival mode. It means slowly teaching your body and mind that staying present is safe - rebuilding tolerance for sensations one layer at a time, so you no longer have to leave yourself behind to survive.

Final Thoughts on Protective Interrupts

Protective interrupts are not signs of weakness, failure, or immaturity. They are evidence of an incredibly sophisticated survival system that learned to prioritise safety above all else. In abuse, the cost of authentic emotional expression can be unthinkably high - so your nervous system adapted. It built detours and emergency exits that allowed you to survive the moment, even if they left the full road of your emotions unfinished.

The difficulty is that these adaptations don't switch off automatically once the threat is gone. The same detours that kept you safe start to keep you stuck. Your body and mind continue running the "abuse-era" version of the emotional cycle, substituting survival scripts where authentic expression should be. That's why even in safe environments you may feel threatened, or find it difficult to access joy, connection, or vulnerability.

Recovery means recognising these interrupts for what they are: a map of where you've been, not a judgement on who you are. The task is not to bulldoze them away, but to retrain your system to trust that authentic emotions can rise, be expressed, and be resolved without harm. That often means:

- Noticing when you hit an interrupt point.
- Creating micro-moments of safety to stay in the cycle a little longer.
- Practising new endings to familiar sequences, so memory begins retrieving healthy, complete cycles instead of survival scripts.

It isn't a quick swap. It's a gradual retraining - convincing your nervous system that the world it once prepared for is not the world you live in now. The old cycle kept you alive. The new one will let you live as your full, authentic self.

Abuser-Driven Hijacks

What They Do To Your Processing Cycle

If protective interrupts are the emergency brakes you pull to keep yourself safe, abuser-driven hijacks are the hands that reach in and rewire the system itself.

Where your adaptations are about survival, theirs are about domination. An abusive partner doesn't just want to control what you do - they often seek to control what you feel, how you express it, and even how you remember feeling it afterwards. Some do this deliberately, others by instinct, but the outcome is the same: your emotional cycle no longer runs freely.

These hijacks are not passive by-products of conflict. They are active interventions, deliberately or repetitively imposed to distort the sequence. Steps are cut out. Meanings are rewritten. False lessons are wired in so consistently that you start to believe them as your own. This doesn't just interrupt single emotions - it reshapes your whole

emotional landscape, training you to swap authenticity for compliance, mistrust your instincts, and doubt the truth of your own experience.

The aim is not only to win the moment, but to ensure the next one is already rigged. By the time a similar situation arises, you've been primed to react on their terms - without them needing to say a word. That is the deepest layer of emotional control: rewriting the source code of your inner life so your feelings, expressions, and even memories are run by them, not you.

5. Flooding / Overwhelm

"They Swamp The System"

Flooding is an abuser-driven hijack where they deliberately overload your emotional processing cycle so you can't keep up. Instead of one manageable spark, they unleash a torrent of accusations, insults, or demands in rapid succession. Each new hit arrives before you've had a chance to register the last one, pushing you past your processing capacity.

In a healthy interaction, people give space for emotional exchange - a rhythm where you can hear, think, respond, and resolve. Flooding deliberately breaks that rhythm. It's a strategy to knock you off balance, prevent you from forming a coherent response, and push you into a reactive state. By saturating your mind and nervous system, they short-circuit your ability to process each moment in sequence.

This isn't always about the scale of the current event. Sometimes, what's flooding you is a combination of now and then - the present spark plus a rush of old, unprocessed emotions that see the current moment as their chance to be felt. Without recognising this, you might misread the intensity as proof the current situation is more dangerous or high-stakes than it really is.

This tactic works because the emotional processing cycle depends on a degree of order. You need time to move from recognition, to sense-making, to expression, to resolution. Flooding collapses those steps into a blur, where recognition is still happening when another blow lands, and sense-making is interrupted before it can take shape. The result is that you end up in a state of confusion, exhaustion, and self-doubt - often agreeing to things, apologising, or shutting down just to make it stop.

Flooding can condition you to give in quickly or stay silent from the outset, just to avoid the onslaught. It becomes a pre-emptive self-defence - but one that costs you your voice, your boundaries, and your ability to stand in your truth.

How Flooding / Overwhelm Works As A Process:

- Step 1 – Spark initiated → Abuser raises a topic, often with a loaded tone, baiting comment, or sudden grievance.
- Step 2 – Escalation → Multiple emotional hits delivered in quick succession - accusations, insults, stacked grievances.
- Step 3 – Processing bottleneck → Your memory and cognition try to track and respond, but each attempt is interrupted mid-cycle.
- Step 4 – System overload → Emotional arousal spikes; fight/flight/freeze/fawn reflexes activate.
- Steps 5–6 – Short-circuited → Sense-making and learning cannot occur; survival mode takes their place.
- Step 7 – False storage → The experience is logged not as clarity, but as fatigue, confusion, and learned compliance.

When your system is repeatedly swamped, the lesson you internalise is not "this was wrong" but "I can't keep up." Exhaustion replaces clarity, and silence replaces resistance. The abuser doesn't need to win arguments with evidence - they win by sheer volume, by teaching you that standing your ground is too costly to attempt.

Left unchecked, flooding undermines individual moments; it rewrites your relationship to conflict itself, leaving you primed to doubt, retreat, or surrender before you've even had the chance to speak.

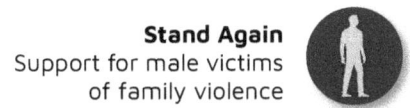

6. Misattribution & Meaning-Rewrite

"They Gaslight You"

Misattribution and meaning-rewrite is one of the most insidious hijacks because it doesn't just shut down your feelings in the moment - it rewrites your internal record of reality. This isn't about debating facts. It's about invalidating the very legitimacy of your emotional response.

You feel sadness, anger, or fear rising - and as your mind begins connecting that feeling to the situation in front of you, the abuser steps in. They insist the meaning you've attached is wrong: *"You're overreacting." "I didn't do anything wrong." "You're too sensitive."* The message is clear: your emotional compass is broken, and only they can provide the "true" reading.

This tactic attacks the cycle at its most fragile point: steps 5 and 6 - sense-making and learning. By hijacking here, they corrupt what gets stored in step 7. And once the record is altered, step 3 - memory recall - will retrieve the corrupted version next time. You aren't just doubting this single moment; you're primed to question every future spark of emotion before it's even finished forming.

This creates an emotional echo chamber where their narrative drowns out your own. The longer it continues, the harder it becomes to distinguish between your authentic reactions and the rewrites they've implanted. The cost isn't just confusion - it's the gradual erosion of self-trust, leaving you dependent on their framing to tell you what's real.

How Misattribution & Meaning Rewrite Hijacks The Cycle:

- Step 1 – Spark detected → An event triggers an authentic emotional response.
- Step 2–3 – Memory recall → Past experiences are pulled in to help interpret it.
- Step 4 – Early expression → Body language, tone, or words begin to show your feeling.

- Step 5 – Hijack during sense-making → They interrupt, questioning or denying the validity of your emotion.
- Step 6 – Meaning rewrite → They supply their narrative, framing you as wrong, unstable, or unreasonable.
- Step 7 – Altered storage → The manipulated version becomes what's logged.
- Future recall → At the next spark, your mind retrieves *their* rewrite - priming you to mistrust your own feelings.

The danger of misattribution and meaning-rewrite is that it erodes the foundation of self-trust. When your feelings are constantly reframed as wrong or illegitimate, you stop believing your own emotional compass. You don't just question what happened - you question your right to feel at all. This makes you easier to control, because every future spark of emotion is already compromised by self-doubt. The risk is not only that you carry their version of events in your memory, but that you begin to live by it, shaping your reactions and even your identity around their narrative instead of your truth.

7. Window-Of-Tolerance Conditioning

"They Get You Used To Abuse"

Expanding your window of tolerance is one of the abuser's most subtle, yet devastating manipulations. It doesn't rely on sudden explosions or dramatic cruelty. Instead, it works like a slow drip - a steady erosion of what you believe is acceptable. What once felt intolerable begins to feel "normal," not because it is, but because you've been trained to adjust one step at a time.

In the emotional processing cycle, this conditioning targets step 3: memory recall. Each time you encounter harm or disrespect, your mind instinctively compares it to past experiences to gauge how to react. The abuser exploits this mechanism. They escalate in increments, ensuring that when your mind looks back, it finds something only slightly less severe than today. The result is that you don't experience the jolt of alarm that might otherwise trigger boundaries or resistance.

It's the psychological equivalent of turning up the heat slowly. If they jumped from sarcasm to screaming overnight, you'd see the danger clearly. But stretched over months or years - from sarcasm, to criticism, to belittling, to outright contempt - the slope is gradual enough to keep you in place. By the time the water is boiling, you've been conditioned to sit still.

This conditioning rewrites the emotional cycle itself. In step 3, instead of recalling the healthy boundaries you once held, you recall last week's "slightly worse" event - and use that as your reference point. Your authentic self, the one who would have walked away at the first sign of harm, gets overwritten by a conditioned self trained to endure. What feels like "strength" in the moment is actually a systematic dismantling of your ability to act on your own truth.

How Window-Of-Tolerance Conditioning Hijacks The Cycle:

- Step 1 – Spark detected → A triggering event occurs, causing emotional discomfort.
- Step 2–3 – Compare to past → Your mind recalls a recent similar event that was only slightly less harmful.
- Minimisation → "It's not that much worse than last time."
- Step 4–5 – Endurance → You mute your authentic response and choose to endure.
- Step 6 – Incremental escalation → The abuser raises the level of harm again, just past your current limit.
- Step 7 – Memory update → The new, slightly worse event becomes your fresh reference point.
- Baseline shift → Over multiple cycles, your tolerance expands far beyond healthy limits.

The danger of window-of-tolerance conditioning is that it teaches you to live smaller without realising it. By the time you notice something is wrong, your baseline for "normal" has already been shifted so far that it's almost unrecognisable. You no longer react to disrespect, cruelty, or even outright abuse the way you once would, because your nervous system has been trained to treat it as tolerable. The risk is not just that you endure harm longer than you should - it's that you begin to doubt your right to expect anything better.

Recovery means rebuilding those boundaries from the ground up, learning again where your true limits lie, and trusting that you are not unreasonable for holding them.

8. Cue → Response Conditioning

"They Train Your Emotional Responses"

Cue → response training is where the abuser conditions you to have a predictable emotional reaction to a specific stimulus - without needing to go through the full abuse each time. It's classic Pavlovian conditioning, but with an added layer of plausible deniability so they can dismiss your reaction as irrational or "over the top."

In the emotional processing cycle, this hijack is designed to short-circuit steps 1-4 entirely. Instead of moving from spark → sensation → meaning → memory, your brain skips straight to the conditioned emotion. Eventually, the cue itself becomes enough to trigger the response, even if the actual threat doesn't follow.

It works like this: the abuser repeatedly pairs a neutral or ambiguous cue - such as slamming a door, a particular tone of voice, or even a sigh - with a negative emotional experience (e.g. rage, humiliation, or intimidation).

At first, you feel the full emotional processing cycle:

- Step 1: The door slams (spark)
- Step 2: You feel your heart race (sensation)
- Step 3: You recall past door slams leading to fights (memory)
- Step 4: You brace for what's coming (expression preparation)

But repetition rewires the system. Now the door slam *is* the threat. Your body reacts instantly, skipping steps 2-4 altogether. The cycle has been rewritten so that the cue alone delivers the emotional state the abuser

wants - fear, compliance, appeasement - without them lifting another finger.

The "plausible deniability" part is what keeps you off-balance. If you react to the cue, they can act innocent: "I didn't mean anything by it," "It was just the wind," "You're so sensitive." This not only deepens self-doubt, but also allows them to reframe your reaction as the problem - shifting blame back onto you.

How Cue → Response Conditioning Works As A Process:

- Step 1 (Spark) → A neutral cue appears (door slam, sigh, clipped tone).
- Step 2 (Sensation) → At first, you feel a natural surge of emotional arousal.
- Step 3 (Memory Recall) → Early on, you connect the cue with past harm. In time, the cue alone becomes the memory.
- Step 4 (Expression) → The body skips authentic expression, moving straight into fear, appeasement, or withdrawal.
- Step 5-7 (Meaning → Learning → Storage) → The manipulated lesson is stored: "this cue = danger." Each repetition deepens the association.

The danger of cue → response conditioning is that it lasts long after the abuser is gone. Long after the relationship ends, ordinary sounds or gestures can still send your body into a survival state, as if the abuse were happening all over again. This not only robs you of safety in the present, but also convinces you that your instincts can't be trusted. Recovery means retraining the cycle - teaching your nervous system that a slam can be just a slam, a sigh just a sigh, and that your emotions belong to you again.

Final Thoughts On Abuser-Driven Hijacks

Abuser-driven hijacks are about rewriting your emotional processing cycle so it no longer belongs to you. These tactics aren't random or clumsy - they're deliberate, patterned interventions designed to shape how you feel, how you express it, and even how you remember those feelings later.

Where protective interrupts are survival adaptations you create to keep yourself safe, hijacks are intrusions. They step into the middle of your natural emotional sequence and insert new instructions - sometimes subtly, sometimes aggressively - until the original pathway is overwritten. Those instructions stop feeling like "what they made me do" and start feeling like "what I do." That's when the conditioning has taken root.

The goal is always twofold:

1. **Control in the moment** - steering or shutting down your immediate emotional response so you stay manageable and compliant.
2. **Control in the future** - training you to respond their way automatically, so they can get the reaction they want without visible effort.

The danger is that once these hijacks are embedded, the abuser doesn't even need to be in the room for them to work. A tone of voice, a slammed door, a familiar phrase - all of it can light up the same cycle, sending you into fear, withdrawal, or appeasement as if they were standing right beside you. This is how abuse leaves an imprint that outlives the relationship, carried in your body and mind long after the abuser is gone.

Breaking these hijacks means reclaiming ownership of each stage of the cycle. It requires learning to spot when a feeling has been planted, rewritten, or short-circuited - and then deliberately running the full, healthy cycle through to completion. At first, this feels forced, even unnatural, because you are building new neural and emotional pathways against years of conditioning. But with practice, the balance shifts. Their instructions fade, your authentic responses strengthen, and step by step, your emotions become yours again.

How Abuse Hijacks the Emotional Processing Cycle
The interrupts that cause disruption to the normal processing of emotional experiences

Step 1 — Something Happens
An event happens, traumatic memory resurfaces, or false narrative internalised

Step 2 — It Sparks an Emotion
Emotional response triggered

Step 3 — Memory Recall & Conditioning
Your **brain pulls up distorted memories from abuse.** Past punishments for certain feelings override the present moment, flooding you with old fear or shame.

Step 4 — Internal Sensation & External Expression
- Internal sensations (tight chest, warm glow)
- Outward expression (smiling, crying).

Are out of sync with

You may feel anxious but smile, or feel sadness but show no emotion — masking to stay safe

Step 5 — Sense-Making
Your **mind is hijacked by the abuser's narrative** — you doubt your feelings, question your right to feel them, or reframe them as your fault

Step 6 — Learning
Instead of learning healthy lessons, **you reinforce survival strategies** like silence, appeasement, or emotional suppression.

Step 7 — Storing
Your brain **stores the distorted pattern.** Over time, it becomes the default, making healthy emotional processing harder to access.

Distorted Memory Stored for Later Recall

Stand Again
Support for male victims of family violence

Copyright © 2026 Stand Again

What Happens if This Remains Broken

When the emotional processing cycle remains hijacked or interrupted for long enough, the effects don't just appear in isolated moments - they begin to shape your entire emotional landscape. Instead of emotions rising, moving through you, and resolving naturally, they either spill out unpredictably, overwhelm you with intensity, or vanish into numbness.

Three of the most common outcomes for survivors are **emotional dysregulation**, **emotional dissociation**, and **mood lability**. These aren't character flaws or emotional weakness - they are nervous system adaptations to prolonged stress. In an abusive environment, they may have been the only way you could survive. In recovery, though, they become barriers to connection, self-trust, and healing.

1. Emotional Dysregulation

Emotional dysregulation happens when your responses no longer match the size, timing, or nature of what's in front of you. The feeling comes in too much or too little, too fast or too late. It might burst out like a balloon overfilled, or collapse suddenly like one with no air left.

In a healthy emotional cycle, feelings rise and fall in proportion to the spark. You have space to sense, name, and act on them in a way that fits the moment. In a hijacked cycle, the survival brain takes over - either flooding you with activation or shutting you down before the cycle is complete. The result isn't balance; it's volatility.

Many of the abuser-driven hijacks feed this volatility:

- **Flooding / overwhelm** trains your balloon to pop under pressure, as too many hits land at once.

- **Cue → response conditioning** wires you to inflate instantly at a small cue, whether danger is present or not.
- **Gaslighting and meaning rewrite** twist your sense-making, so the balloon bursts sideways into shame or self-blame instead of authentic expression.
- **Window-stretching** stretches your tolerance so far that the balloon walls become thin and fragile - unable to hold pressure safely.

Dysregulation can feel like:

- Exploding in anger over something small, then feeling ashamed afterwards.
- Feeling flat in moments where you know you should be moved.
- Switching emotional gears without warning - calm one moment, in tears the next.
- Feeling like your emotions are bursting out of your hands.
- Watching yourself unravel in real time, unable to steer.

Dysregulation erodes trust in yourself. You can't predict whether you'll under-react, over-react, or collapse altogether. That unpredictability makes it harder to show up in line with your values - and harder for others to understand you, even when your care and intent are genuine.

2. Emotional Dissociation

Emotional dissociation is what happens when a temporary survival bypass becomes a permanent fixture. In the abuse itself, dissociation shows up as a hijack - a moment where your system cuts the link between sensation and awareness to keep you from being overwhelmed. That's the *dissociative bypass*. But when this survival manoeuvre is repeated often enough, it doesn't stay situational. It becomes the default wiring. Emotional dissociation is the long-term state where access to your own emotions is dulled, muted, or missing altogether - not just in dangerous moments, but across your whole life.

You might still be feeling something somewhere in your body, but it never fully arrives in your conscious mind - or if it does, it's foggy, distant, and strangely disconnected from the moment you're in. Joy, grief, anger, even love can all feel like they're happening behind a sheet of glass.

Dissociation can feel like:

- Watching your own life like it's on a screen, rather than participating in it.
- Struggling to feel joy, grief, or anger even when the situation calls for it.
- Feeling like the "volume" of emotions is turned down or muted.
- Experiencing physical symptoms (tight chest, stomach knots) but not recognising them as connected to an emotion.
- Losing chunks of memory from moments where emotions should have been high.

In the short term, this response was protective. It shielded you from unbearable overwhelm when you couldn't escape. But in the long term, it blunts your ability to connect - both with yourself and with others. Relationships suffer because connection requires presence, and presence requires access to your emotional signals. Recovery becomes harder, too, because without full access to your feelings, you can't process them all the way through. Healing gets stuck half-finished.

3. Mood Lability

Mood lability is what happens when your emotional system swings unpredictably between extremes - sometimes flooding you with feelings that feel too big for the moment, other times cutting you off from feelings altogether. It's not steady, and it's not predictable. One minute you may be calm, the next you're overwhelmed with grief or rage, and then suddenly flat and detached.

This instability develops because the emotional processing cycle has been so distorted that it can't find balance. In one moment, the system

might over-fire (like in dysregulation), pouring out emotions in a tidal wave. In the next, it might under-fire (like in dissociation), shutting everything down to avoid danger. Instead of running a smooth rhythm of spark → feeling → sense-making → resolution, the cycle oscillates chaotically, flipping between states that don't match the situation you're in.

Mood lability can feel like:

- Crying intensely, then feeling strangely numb minutes later.
- Jumping from anger to guilt to shame in rapid succession without clarity on why.
- Feeling unpredictable even to yourself, wondering "Which version of me will show up today?"
- Struggling to explain reactions to others because they shift so quickly.
- Relationships becoming strained because your emotional presence feels unstable or inconsistent.

Mood lability creates its own kind of exhaustion. Instead of trusting your emotional compass, you live braced for swings you can't control. This undermines confidence in your own stability, making it harder to build secure relationships or feel grounded in daily life.

Mood lability is different from dysregulation or dissociation alone because it's not just "too much" or "too little." It's the unpredictable movement between them - the nervous system trying and failing to find a middle ground. In many survivors, it becomes the ongoing "default state," where emotions are always shifting, but rarely resolving.

Repairing The Emotional Processing Cycle

Rebuilding after abuse isn't just about leaving the situation.

It's about reclaiming your internal systems so they work for you again. One of the most important - and most overlooked - of these systems is your emotional processing cycle. When it's intact, the cycle acts like a finely tuned guidance system: it detects when something is wrong, helps you name what you're feeling, and moves you towards an action or resolution that protects and connects you.

In an abusive environment, that system isn't just disrupted - it's often rewired. Like faulty wiring behind a wall, the connections are tampered with until the current no longer runs cleanly from spark to resolution. Emotions are hijacked so often that the circuit diverts, loops, shuts down, or ends in an outcome that doesn't truly belong to you. You may react in ways that once kept you physically safe in the moment, but now leave you emotionally stuck long after.

This matters because recovery isn't only about avoiding more harm - it's about creating a life where your emotional signals are both trustworthy and usable. If the wiring stays faulty, it becomes harder to tell the difference between a genuine warning and a conditioned reflex. You might freeze or fawn when you actually need to assert yourself. You might downplay hurt because you've been trained to believe it isn't valid. Or you might feel emotion rising with no idea what to do with it, except push it back down.

What follows is not a prescription but a scaffold. Every survivor's wiring has its own variations, and not every repair technique will fit every situation. The aim is to give you a starting map - practical ways to respond when you notice a short-circuit pulling you off-course. From there, you can adapt the approach to your own nervous system, your own triggers, and your own pace.

Restoring the cycle is critical because it reconnects you to your internal compass. It allows you to trust that when something feels wrong, the signal is yours - not something installed, rewritten, or suppressed by someone else. It also frees you to experience emotions fully without

being ruled by them. Instead of avoiding feelings because they once led to danger, you can let them guide you to clarity and resolution.

Recovery isn't just about getting your life back. It's about getting your self back. And repairing the emotional cycle - one wire at a time - is one of the clearest pathways to do it.

What To Expect During Repair

Rebuilding your emotional processing cycle is not light or effortless. At the start, it will feel intense. Sometimes overwhelming. Sometimes even frightening. That's not a sign you're doing it wrong - it's the natural response of a nervous system trained to avoid, bypass, or shut down emotions for survival.

You might:

- Feel more in the early steps, not less, because you're opening channels you've been blocking for years.
- Want to pull back after a few attempts, because staying with feelings you once had to avoid can feel confronting.
- Struggle with inconsistency - a shift works for a day or two, then the old wiring pulls you back.
- Judge yourself harshly for "falling back" into suppression, freezing, or other survival adaptations.

As you begin this work, backlog emotions can break through suddenly. Because you're creating space to feel again, your nervous system may treat it as an opening for unprocessed emotions to surface. This can feel disproportionate to the moment, but it's simply old wires trying to complete a circuit that never closed.

You may also notice yourself doubling down on old behaviours in safe relationships. This often happens when you care deeply about a new person and desperately want to "get it right." Without realising it, you lean harder on survival responses that once kept you safe in abuse - appeasement, self-suppression, over-accommodation. In an abusive context, these tactics reduced harm. In a healthy relationship, they create distance or tension, because they bypass authentic emotional connection.

This is all part of reintegration. Repair doesn't happen in a straight line - it's a process of rewiring, one connection at a time.

Think of it like repairing a circuit after an electrical fire:

- You start with small, deliberate fixes.
- You test them, again and again, until they hold.
- You gradually restore more connections and strength.

If you push too hard, your system will trip the breaker. If you go steady, your system has time to trust the new patterns you're building. Eventually, the cycle that once defaulted to survival begins defaulting to healthy completion.

The goal here isn't perfection - it's progress. You're retraining your body and mind to handle emotions in real time, without being ruled by them or trapped by faulty wiring.

When To Get Professional Support

This work can be done on your own. But not always. Some signs indicate you need a trauma-informed therapist or coach alongside you, not just a book:

- **Dissociation you can't pull out of.** If you find yourself zoning out for extended periods and grounding techniques don't bring you back, that's beyond self-work.

- **Flashbacks that intensify.** Some memory surfacing is normal. Flashbacks that get worse, more vivid, or more frequent as you do this work need professional containment.

- **Inability to function.** If you can't get through basic daily tasks — work, caring for yourself or your kids, eating, sleeping — the repair work is destabilising you faster than you can stabilise.

- **Persistent panic or overwhelm.** A spike of anxiety is expected. Panic attacks that don't resolve, or a sense of dread that doesn't lift, need more support than a book can provide.

- **Thoughts of self-harm.** Full stop. If these arise, pause the work and reach out to a professional or crisis service immediately.

- **Getting worse, not better.** Progress isn't linear, but the overall direction should be toward stability. If you're consistently feeling worse over weeks of practice, something needs adjusting with qualified guidance.

There's no shame in needing support. These patterns were laid down under extreme conditions. Some wiring needs a professional hand to repair safely.

How To Recondition Emotional Processing

There are many ways to repair and recondition your emotional processing cycle. Some therapies and practices are designed to target specific points in the cycle - like calming the nervous system (regulating the power source), accessing stored memory safely (testing a blocked wire), or journaling to make sense of emotions (rewiring the meaning circuit).

Some popular practices include:

- **EMDR (Eye Movement Desensitisation and Reprocessing):** helps the brain safely reprocess traumatic memories.
- **Somatic Experiencing:** builds tolerance for body sensations linked to past overwhelm.

- **IFS (Internal Family Systems):** gives voice to "parts" of you that carry trauma and restores balance between them.
- **Schema Therapy:** challenges long-standing survival beliefs and replaces them with healthier wiring.
- **Breathwork and Yoga:** regulate the nervous system by anchoring you back into the body.
- **Journaling or Narrative Therapy:** supports sense-making and storing of experience through story.
- **Safe Relational Practice:** rebuilds trust through supportive, consistent connections.

All of these are valuable. None of them are wrong. Depending on your nervous system, one may feel more effective than another.

Our focus here is on a **step-by-step repair process** you can use to recondition yourself back into a healthy emotional cycle. This method draws on body-first practices, meaning-first practices, and relational repair, but frames them as a clear sequence you can follow - one wire at a time.

Unless your therapist guides you otherwise, you can use this process as your main scaffold. It's not a substitute for therapy, and it doesn't exclude other tools. Use what works for you. If one approach feels more effective than another, lean into that. The important thing is that the cycle begins to run cleanly again - in whatever way helps you get there.

Step-By-Step Reconditioning

To rebuild your emotional cycle, you don't work on everything at once. You take one old pattern - whether it's freezing, shutting down, dismissing yourself, or any other survival reflex - and bring it through the repair steps one wire at a time.

You can't repair them all at once. You rebuild **one wire at a time**.

That means you:

- **Notice** when an old pattern is firing (Step 1: Awareness without action).
- **Create a crack** with a tiny, deliberate self-regulation move (Step 2: Controlled micro-interrupts).
- **Choose the healthy alternative** you will install for this wire (Step 3: Choosing healthy alternatives).
- **Reinforce by repetition** until the new wire holds under mild stress (Step 4: Repetition and reinforcement).
- **Run it live** in everyday interactions so the system self-corrects (Step 5: Integration and expansion).

The good news: once a few wires are repaired, the system starts helping itself. Healthy connections reduce reinforcement of the old loops, and cleaner pathways begin to auto-correct glitches when they appear.

You'll work these **five steps for each specific wire**, not all at once. Each successful repair makes the next one easier - like resetting circuits one by one until the whole board runs cleanly.

Pacing matters. Pushing too far, too fast can overwhelm or re-traumatise. Going too slow - pulling back at the first hint of discomfort - can keep you stuck in old survival loops. Aim to stretch just beyond what's comfortable without tipping into shutdown.

This work isn't about re-living past trauma. It's about meeting the emotions that arise **now**, in response to current experiences, and holding steady with them long enough for the cycle to run cleanly again. That's how your emotional processing becomes safe, fluid, and trustworthy.

Where possible, do this with a trauma-informed coach or therapist, especially if you notice overwhelm, panic, or shutdown as you begin.

Reintegrating the Emotional Processing Cycle
How we carefully and with care reintegrate to our authentic feelings

Stand Again
Support for male victims of family violence

Awareness Without Action

Stage 1

First, you learn to spot when your emotional process is being hijacked or cut short.

This might be a sudden freeze, shutting down, jumping to overthinking, or feeling hijacked by an old emotional script.

You name it in plain terms: "I'm freezing," "I'm overriding," "This is self-suppression."

This stage is about awareness only — not forcing change yet.

Controlled Micro-Interrupts

Stage 2

Choose one small, safe action to complete a missing part of the emotional cycle.

Examples: allow yourself to frown when sad, take two extra breaths before changing the topic, write down one feeling word.

Keep it deliberately small so your nervous system feels safe.

Partial Completion

Stage 3

Now you extend your tolerance a little further than before, without aiming for the full cycle.

If you normally stop at feeling, you add a low-risk expression.

If you normally freeze at sense-making, you write down one sentence of meaning.

This stage teaches your system that it can handle "more" without being overwhelmed.

Full Cycle Completion

Stage 4

You intentionally run the emotion through all stages: spark → feeling → expression → sense-making → learning → storing.

Often starts in private — journaling, talking to yourself, voice notes — before doing it with others.

Here you rebuild trust in your emotions: the signal you start with is the one you finish with.

Real-Time Integration

Stage 4

You can run a clean cycle in the moment, even with others present and mild stress in the mix.

You catch hijack attempts (internal or external) as they happen and redirect instantly.

In healthy relationships, this stage means learning to dial back old survival patterns — like over-appeasing or overexplaining — and letting authentic emotion be part of the exchange.

Copyright © 2026 Stand Again

Step 1 - Awareness Without Action

This step is about catching the old wire in the act. Every survival adaptation - whether it shows up as a thought, a body signal, or a behaviour - needs to be noticed before it can be reconditioned.

When an old wire fires, it often feels so quick and automatic that you only notice it afterwards. That's because these patterns weren't chosen - they were drilled in under pressure. They were laid down in moments when you needed to survive, and so they became reflexes. Reflexes don't ask permission. They run invisibly in the background, shaping how you think, feel, and act before you've even realised it. Awareness is the first time you bring them into the light.

How The Old Wiring Shows Up

Every survivor's wiring looks slightly different, but there are common patterns that cut across most experiences. Learning to recognise them is like learning to spot the flicker of a faulty light bulb - once you see the flicker, you can't unsee it.

- **Suppression** - pushing feelings down before they ever reach expression. It often comes with inner commands like *"don't start this now"* or *"it's not worth the fight."* On the outside, it looks like calm. On the inside, it's a lock being thrown across the door of your emotions.
- **Fawning** - abandoning your own truth to soothe someone else. You smile, nod, or agree even when you feel differently, because harmony feels safer than honesty. Fawning doesn't just smooth conflict - it erases your voice until you forget what your real response was meant to be.
- **Dissociation** - going blank or switching off, so emotions don't even register in real time. It can feel like floating above yourself, staring through the moment, or suddenly being absent from your own body. Later you realise something important happened - but you weren't really there for it.

- **Over-control** - talking yourself into restraint, managing, analysing, or intellectualising so you don't have to touch the rawness of feeling. It feels responsible, composed, rational. But underneath, it's just another way of keeping emotions at arm's length.
- **Avoidance behaviours** - changing the subject, laughing it off, distracting yourself with work or screens. It can look social, light, or productive. But each time, it's a detour away from the emotion that was about to surface.

Where It Cuts The Cycle

These faulty wires don't just appear anywhere - they tend to hijack the emotional process at predictable points. Think of the emotional cycle like a current running through a circuit: feeling → expression → sense-making → storage. A bad wire cuts in and shuts the flow down.

- **Before expression** - the feeling sparks but is immediately suppressed. You feel the swell in your chest, the words on your tongue, the heat in your body... but then the door slams shut. Nothing is spoken, nothing is shown. The emotion is stopped before it has a chance to breathe.
- **Before sense-making** - the emotion surfaces but gets bypassed before you can reflect on it. The fear, the anger, the sadness flickers through you - but then it's shoved aside or numbed out before you can ask, *"What is this telling me?"* It's like a book you open but never read.
- **Before storage** - you actually allow yourself to feel it, maybe even think about what it means, but then you erase it in the final stage. You dismiss it as irrelevant, deny it as weakness, or bury it so it won't leave a trace. The experience never gets stored as something completed or integrated - it lingers as open, unfinished business.

Knowing where the short-circuit happens is crucial. Suppressing before expression requires a different kind of repair than erasing after storage. One is about opening the door to feeling. The other is about keeping the door open long enough for the experience to settle and belong to you.

The Practice Of Awareness

At this step, you are not trying to correct, replace, or fight the reflex. That comes later. For now, the task is simple but powerful: to **see the wire clearly, mark it, and let it go**.

1. **Notice it firing.** Catch the moment the old wiring switches on. It might be subtle - the tightening of your chest, the sudden urge to go quiet, the way your mind scrambles for a distraction. The key is not to change it, but to witness it. Every time you notice, you bring what was unconscious into the light.
2. **Label it clearly.** Put words to what you're doing: *"I'm fawning." "I'm suppressing." "That's old thinking."* The label is not an insult - it's a map. By naming the wire itself, you take something that once ran invisibly and pin it down where you can see it.
3. **Release it.** Once you've caught and named it, consciously mark it as old: *"I see you, and I let you go."* This step is not about forcing the pattern away - it's about signalling to your nervous system that awareness has been achieved. The reflex doesn't have to keep running invisibly in the background.

Awareness works like switching on a light in a dark room. Nothing about the furniture changes, but suddenly you can see where everything is. This clarity is what makes repair possible in the steps ahead.

The Practice of Reflection

Sometimes the old wire fires and finishes before awareness catches up. The fawn completes. The shutdown runs its course. The suppression locks in. You only realise what happened afterwards — minutes, hours, sometimes days later.

This is normal. These patterns were drilled in under threat, thousands of times. They were designed to fire fast. Catching them after the fact doesn't mean you're failing at recovery — it means you're paying attention.

The temptation is to turn on yourself. "Why did I do that again?" "I should know better by now." That voice sounds like accountability, but it's not. It's the old wiring dressed up as self-improvement — the same voice that told you your feelings were wrong, your reactions too much, your instincts not to be trusted.

Don't beat yourself up. Take it as an opportunity to learn more about your faulty wiring.

Reflection isn't punishment. It's examination:

1. **Identify the wire.** What pattern fired? Was it suppression? Fawning? Dissociation? Over-control? Name it plainly, without judgement.

2. **Locate the cut.** Where did it interrupt the cycle? Did it stop before expression? Before sense-making? Before storage? Knowing where the circuit broke tells you what needs repair.

3. **Trace the trigger.** What sparked it? A tone of voice? A feeling of being cornered? A reminder of something old? The trigger isn't always obvious — sometimes it's layered beneath the surface.

4. **Note without shame.** Write it down or speak it aloud. "Today I fawned when my friend pushed back on my idea. The wire cut before I could voice what I actually thought." That's data, not verdict.

Every reflection adds to the map. Each entry sharpens your understanding of how your wiring operates — what fires, when, and why. Over time, that map makes awareness faster. The wire that once ran invisibly becomes something you recognise sooner. And eventually, before it finishes.

Why Awareness Matters

It's tempting to skip this step. Survivors of abuse are conditioned to scan for threats, find fast fixes, and leap straight into action. Doing nothing can feel unsafe, even irresponsible. But without awareness as your foundation, every attempt at repair rests on shaky ground.

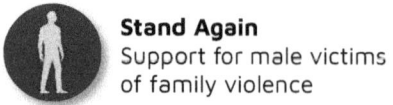

Stand Again
Support for male victims
of family violence

Without awareness you risk:

- **Misdiagnosis** - replacing the wrong wire because you didn't see what was actually firing. You end up working on the symptom, not the source.
- **Overwhelm** - trying to "fix" too many things at once without clarity. The nervous system becomes flooded and shuts down.
- **Reinforcement** - pushing harder against a reflex can strengthen it, teaching the body that the old survival pattern is still required.

Awareness without action slows everything down. It interrupts the instinct to rush. Think of it as taking a highlighter to the blueprint of your wiring - marking the faulty circuits before you ever touch a tool. In that pause, you create the space where change can later take root.

Practices That Help

Awareness is a skill, not an instinct. At first, it feels elusive. The reflex fires so quickly you barely register it. But each time you pause to notice, you slow the wiring just enough to see its shape. These practices anchor that pause and make it repeatable:

- **Body-first:** somatic tracking, pausing to notice sensations without changing them, placing a hand on your chest or stomach as you name and release. These simple physical anchors remind your body that you are safe enough to observe without reacting. By noticing without interference, you train your nervous system to sit with sensation rather than collapse into suppression or avoidance.
- **Meaning-first:** journaling or voice notes, writing down exactly what you noticed and the release you gave it: "Today I caught myself suppressing. I said I see it, and I let it go." Putting the reflex into words transfers it from the shadows into memory. This builds a visible record of your wiring - proof that the once-

invisible reflex is now something you can reliably catch in the light.

The goal of Step 1 is not correction - it's exposure. Once the unconscious reflex is visible, labelled, and released, it begins to lose its invisibility cloak. Each act of noticing softens the automatic hold, and each release makes room for a new response. From here, the work of repair can truly begin.

Step 2 - Controlled Micro-Interrupts

Once you've mapped an old wire, the next step is to insert the smallest possible change into its pathway - a micro-interrupt.

You're not trying to rebuild the entire cycle yet. You're simply testing the circuit. Think of it as creating a hairline crack in the reflex so that light can get in. These interruptions don't replace the wiring, but they expose the fact that it can be shifted.

Micro-interrupts you choose from (pick what works for you):

- Take one slow, grounding breath before you act.
- Relax your hands instead of clenching them.
- Soften your jaw when you feel it tightening.
- Drop your shoulders when you notice them rising.
- Add a single sentence before you default to silence.
- Ask one clarifying question instead of immediately appeasing.
- Make a quick note in your phone before you push a feeling down.
- Say a short phrase to yourself: *"Old wire, not current threat."*
- Change your posture - sit back in the chair rather than leaning forward.
- Give yourself three seconds of pause before answering.

The point isn't to dismantle the whole reflex. It's to catch it early and nudge it slightly off track. A survival adaptation that once felt like a locked circuit - automatic and unbreakable - shows itself to have space for interruption. That small nudge is enough to prove that the reflex is not absolute.

Why Micro?

If you try to rewire everything at once, your nervous system will resist. These old patterns are not random habits - they were survival mechanisms. They formed under pressure, and in those moments they worked. They once kept you safe, or at least safer, than the alternative. To your system, abandoning them completely still feels like walking into danger.

That's why change has to begin small. A micro-interrupt is tiny enough to slip past the alarm bells, but significant enough to prove a new pathway exists. It's a safe experiment, a way of showing your body that deviation no longer leads to catastrophe.

During abuse, deviation came at a cost: punishment, rage, withdrawal, or danger. The nervous system learned that any break from the script invited harm. Even now, long after the abuse, that memory lingers. The body remembers what change once cost, so even harmless deviations can feel threatening.

Micro-interrupts work because they respect that memory. They don't try to rip the wiring out. They create a controlled crack - a deliberate pause or shift that teaches the system something new: *"This time, nothing bad happened."* These small experiments accumulate. The reflex loses its grip, and your body begins to trust that it is safe enough to choose differently.

Common Pitfalls

It's easy to mistake the purpose of micro-interrupts and fall into old survival habits disguised as "progress." Some of the most common traps are:

- **Going too big, too fast.** Trying to change everything at once feels productive, but it overwhelms the nervous system. Instead

of safety, you end up triggering the same shutdown or panic you're trying to rewire.
- **Expecting instant results.** A micro-interrupt is not designed to "fix" the pattern overnight. Its role is to build tolerance and trust in small deviations. Measuring success too quickly only fuels frustration.
- **Judging the attempt.** Survivors are conditioned to measure themselves against impossible standards. If you see a micro-interrupt as "not enough," you miss its value. The point is not perfection, but practice.
- **Treating it like performance.** A micro-interrupt is not something you "get right" for others to see. It's an internal shift - proof to your own nervous system that a different path is available.
- **Confusing suppression with progress.** Forcing yourself not to feel or overriding the reflex with sheer willpower is not the same as interrupting it. Suppression keeps the wire hidden. A micro-interrupt brings it into the open.

The key is remembering what this step is for: you are not rebuilding the whole system yet. You are testing the wiring, gently showing yourself that even the smallest crack in the reflex makes space for something new.

What You're Really Doing

A micro-interrupt isn't about fixing the reflex in one move. It doesn't erase the old wiring or instantly create a new one. What it does is build **tolerance for difference**. Each small interruption is a deliberate act of self-regulation - proof to your nervous system that a deviation, however minor, no longer leads to catastrophe.

In survival mode, your system learned that deviation was dangerous. Pausing, speaking, showing emotion - all of these once carried a cost. The reflexes you developed ran automatically because they had to. By introducing micro-interrupts, you're teaching your body that difference is now safe.

With repetition, the effect compounds:

- **The reflex slows.** What once fired instantly begins to hesitate, giving you a fraction more space.
- **The crack widens.** The small shift you create becomes easier to repeat, and harder for the old pattern to override.
- **Choice returns.** Instead of being carried by the reflex, you begin to insert conscious decision. Even a moment of choice is enough to prove the reflex no longer owns you.

The true value of a micro-interrupt is not in the single act, but in the **accumulation of safety**. Each one is a message to your body: *"I can survive doing this differently now."* Eventually, those messages layer into a new baseline, and the old wiring loses its grip.

Practices That Help

Micro-interrupts only work when they are repeatable and tolerable. The aim isn't to force change but to gently prove that difference is possible without danger. These practices offer concrete ways to experiment:

- **Body-first.** Use physical anchors that signal safety to your nervous system. One slow exhale before responding. Relax your jaw. Drop your shoulders. Open your palms. These gestures are small enough not to feel threatening, but each one interrupts the old wire and reminds your body it is safe to soften.
- **Meaning-first.** Add words or symbols that reframe the reflex. Scripted reminders like, *"This is an old wire, not the present moment,"* create space between past and present. Jotting a single keyword in your phone or notebook before suppressing the thought prevents it from vanishing entirely and keeps it in awareness.
- **Therapy tie-ins.** Somatic experiencing and schema therapy both emphasise titration - making small, tolerable shifts instead of overwhelming the system. Micro-interrupts follow that same principle: the smallest sustainable step forward, repeated often enough to show your nervous system that safety now exists where once there was threat.

The goal of Step 2 is not dramatic breakthrough. It is to prove safety through small deviations. Each micro-interrupt is like testing a door you once believed was permanently bolted shut. At first it shifts only a fraction, then a little more. With practice, the door opens fully, and choice becomes part of your everyday wiring.

Step 3 – Choosing Healthy Alternatives

By now, the groundwork is laid.

- In **Step 1**, you identified and named the old wires - those survival reflexes that once kept you safe but now keep you stuck.
- In **Step 2**, you created small cracks in those reflexes through micro-interrupts, proving that deviation is not only possible but survivable.

Now comes **Step 3: installation**. This is where the real rewiring begins. The nervous system does not leave empty space. If you only disrupt an old reflex without replacing it, the brain will reach back for the most familiar pattern to close the gap. That is why relapse into old responses can feel almost automatic - the wiring is still looking for somewhere to run.

In this stage, you begin deliberately **installing new, healthier alternatives**. Think of it as choosing the counter-move. You are no longer just interrupting the old signal - you are supplying a new one in its place.

This shift requires both precision and intention. It is not about replacing an old reflex with any random behaviour. It is about choosing something that truly moves you toward health, presence, and integrity. Without this step, the cracks made in Step 2 risk collapsing back into the old grooves. With it, those cracks widen into new channels for thought, emotion, and action.

The key is **naming the old wire clearly in the moment**. A micro-interrupt gives you just enough breathing space to ask: *What reflex am I in right now?*

- "I'm suppressing before expression."
- "I'm dissociating before sense-making."
- "I'm fawning instead of being honest."
- "I'm hyper-controlling instead of allowing."

From that naming comes the power to replace. Each time you identify an old reflex, you are standing at a fork in the path. One way leads back to the well-worn track of survival. The other leads to a consciously chosen response - small at first, but carrying the potential to become the new default.

Why replacement matters

A reflex never leaves a vacuum. The nervous system is built to complete circuits, not leave them hanging. If you only interrupt an old reflex but do not install something in its place, the body and mind will automatically reach back for the familiar. The old cycle reasserts itself - not because you failed, but because the brain is designed to conserve energy by running what it already knows.

That is why **replacement is essential**. Interrupts create space, but replacements give that space direction. Each time you choose a healthier alternative - even in the smallest way - you are offering your nervous system a new circuit to fire. Repetition turns that circuit from fragile wiring into a reliable pathway.

Replacement is also where *identity* is reclaimed. This is the moment where you place your hand firmly on the tiller and choose the person you want to become. Instead of being defined by the reflexes installed under abuse, you are writing your own patterns - patterns aligned with honesty, presence, and dignity.

And without this step, the risk isn't only regression. It is **overcorrection**. Survivors who stop at interrupting often slip into new, unhealthy defaults: a blanket distrust of all women, a reflexive rejection of

intimacy, a reliance on control to avoid vulnerability. These are trauma generalisations - protective, yes, but corrosive in the long term. The absence of a healthy replacement leaves space for distorted wiring to take root.

Deliberate replacement prevents that drift. It allows healing to move forward, not sideways. It gives the nervous system not just relief from the old, but a clear alternative to practise until it feels natural. This is where the rewiring truly begins.

Pick A Healthy Alternative (New Wire)

The task is simple in theory but profound in practice: take the reflex that once kept you trapped, and supply a deliberate alternative that moves you toward presence, dignity, and choice.

When it comes to choosing a replacement, you don't have to invent it from thin air. Healthy alternatives can be *borrowed, modelled, or drawn from within*. Think of it like wiring in a new circuit: you can take inspiration from many sources, so long as it leads you toward health and not further into survival reflexes.

Some places you can look for healthy alternatives:

- **Role models**: Notice how someone you respect handles pressure, disagreement, or intimacy. It could be a friend, a mentor, or even a public figure whose qualities resonate with you.
- **Your own values**: Ask yourself, "Who do I want to be in this situation?" The answer doesn't have to be grand - it can be as simple as, "I want to be honest," or "I want to be calm."
- **Stories and characters**: Sometimes a book, film, or even history gives you a model - someone whose integrity or courage you admire.
- **Your future self**: Imagine yourself five years from now, healed and steady. How would that version of you respond?

The key isn't where you find it - the key is whether the replacement *moves you toward health, presence, and integrity.*

Below are some of the most common faulty wirings from abuse, paired with healthier replacements you can begin practising.

Example of healthy alternatives

Faulty Wiring	Old Reflex	Healthy Alternative
Suppression → Expression	Pushing emotions down to avoid conflict, judgement, or "making things worse."	Allow the feeling into the light. Speak it aloud, write it down, or share it with someone you trust. Even naming the emotion to yourself ("I feel sad") is a healthy act of expression.
Dissociation → Grounded Presence	Zoning out, going numb, or detaching from your own body/mind in moments of stress.	Stay anchored in one sensation or layer of feeling. Let yourself feel the *first edge* of the emotion rather than fleeing entirely.
Fawning → Honesty	Abandoning your needs, opinions, or boundaries to appease and keep the peace.	Voice one small truth or assert one boundary, even if it feels uncomfortable. Step toward your own needs instead of erasing them.
Overcontrol → Allowance	Micromanaging every detail to prevent chaos or soothe fear.	Release one small detail and watch what happens. Practise allowing uncertainty without collapse.
Silence → Voice	Withdrawing in conflict or shutting down to avoid escalation.	Offer one clear sentence that keeps you present in the conversation, even if it's as simple as "I need a moment to think."

Faulty Wiring	Old Reflex	Healthy Alternative
Anger (Overreaction) → Discerned Response	Explosive outbursts or total withdrawal when anger is triggered.	Pause long enough to check: Is this righteous anger (protecting dignity) or a reflexive overreaction? Respond in line with the truth of that check.
Shame Spiral → Self-Compassion	Collapsing into "I'm a failure," "I'm not good enough," or carrying unearned guilt.	Reframe with self-kindness: "I made a mistake, but I am not a mistake." Offer yourself the compassion you would extend to a friend.
Hypervigilance → Grounded Awareness	Scanning for threats, reading every silence or gesture as danger.	Remind yourself "This is not then, this is now." Notice the actual environment and choose one cue of safety to rest in.
Emotional Numbing → Safe Engagement	Shutting down joy, affection, or intimacy to avoid being hurt.	Permit one safe moment of positive feeling - a smile, a hug, a laugh - without immediately cutting it off.
Over-Accommodation → Mutuality	Giving more than you receive, feeling responsible for others' emotions.	Practise reciprocity - ask for help, accept care, or let someone else carry part of the load.

Faulty Wiring	Old Reflex	Healthy Alternative
Gaslighting → Trusting Your Own Perception	Second-guessing what you saw, felt, or remembered because it was constantly disputed or denied	Anchor to your direct experience. "This is what I saw. This is what I felt. That's valid." You don't need external validation to make your perception real.
Conditioning Through Criticism → Self-Acceptance	Automatically scanning for mistakes, assuming you're "wrong" or "not enough" before you even act.	Affirm adequacy in the moment: "I'm learning. I'm allowed to be imperfect. My worth is not on trial."
Withholding / Silent Treatment → Self-Connection	Collapsing into panic or shame when cut off emotionally, scrambling to re-establish contact.	Instead of chasing connection, turn inward: ground yourself, self-soothe, and remind yourself "their withdrawal is not proof of my unworthiness."
False Accusations → Anchored Integrity	Reflexively defending yourself against lies, feeling you must over-explain or prove innocence.	Stand in clarity: "I know who I am. I don't have to win their narrative to live my truth." Respond briefly, or not at all, but keep your sense of self intact.
Conditional "Love" → Secure Self-Worth	Tying your value to appeasement, compliance, or meeting their shifting standards.	Practise unconditional self-regard. "My worth does not rise or fall with their approval. I can choose to act from my values, not their conditions."
Fear of Explosion	Appeasing, avoiding, or silencing yourself	Voice one boundary calmly, even if small. Each

Faulty Wiring	Old Reflex	Healthy Alternative
(Walking on Eggshells) → Measured Boundaries	to prevent rage or punishment.	boundary asserted rewires fear into agency.
Learned Helplessness → Agency in Small Steps	Assuming "there's no point," giving up initiative because attempts were punished or undermined.	Take one deliberate action within your control - however small - and acknowledge it. Each act of choice reinforces your capacity.

Each of these alternatives is not about achieving an ideal overnight. They are about building repeatable circuits. The question is always: *What small, healthier choice can I make right now that points me in the direction of who I want to be?*

Install The New Wire

Choosing the healthy alternative is only the beginning. At first, it will feel foreign - even clumsy. That's because your nervous system has been trained to run the old wiring automatically, while the new path is still uncharted.

This stage is about practice. Repetition is what convinces the nervous system that the new pattern is safe, reliable, and worth keeping. Every deliberate attempt sends the message: *this is available, this is survivable, this is who I am becoming.*

Think of it like strengthening a new muscle. The first time you try it, it shakes under the weight. You might wobble, overcorrect, or forget the move halfway through. That isn't failure - it's the process of installation. The body is mapping a new circuit, and it takes time before the signal runs smoothly.

The process looks like this:

- **Expect awkwardness.** The first few times you try a healthier alternative, it may feel forced, mechanical, or even "fake." But fake is only another word for *unfamiliar*. With practice, unfamiliar becomes familiar, and familiar becomes natural. What begins as deliberate eventually becomes default.
- **Rehearse in low-stakes settings.** Practise voicing one sentence with a trusted friend. Practise naming your emotion in a journal before trying it in conversation. Practise holding a boundary in small matters before asserting it in bigger ones. Rehearsal builds fluency so that when the real tests come, the move is already in your body.
- **Prioritise consistency over intensity.** One small, repeatable choice practised daily carries more rewiring power than a single dramatic attempt. Each repetition adds another strand to the new wiring until it is strong enough to carry weight on its own.
- **Return after setbacks.** Falling back into the old reflex doesn't erase the new one. Each time you redirect yourself back to the healthier choice, you strengthen the new circuit further. Reinstallation is progress, not failure.
- **Stabilise through repetition.** With enough practice, the nervous system begins to accept the new wiring as not just possible, but preferable. The old reflex loses its grip - not because you fought it into submission, but because you gave your body and mind a better option to reach for.

Installation is not about perfection - it is about steady practice. Each small attempt, however awkward, is laying track for the new reflex to run on. The rewiring holds when the healthier choice stops feeling like effort and starts feeling like you.

Common Pitfalls In Installing The New Wire

Even with clear intentions, survivors often run into the same traps when practising a healthier alternative. Naming these pitfalls in advance helps you spot them without mistaking them for failure.

- **Mistaking awkwardness for inauthenticity.** The new move feels clumsy at first. That does not mean it's fake or "not really me." It only feels foreign because the old reflex has had more rehearsal.
- **Expecting immediate fluency.** Installation takes repetition. Many give up too soon because the new reflex doesn't "stick" after a handful of tries. Rewiring isn't a single switch - it's a steady layering of practice.
- **All-or-nothing thinking.** Slipping back into the old reflex can trigger shame or despair - *"I'll never change."* In reality, relapse is part of rewiring. Returning to the new move, even after stumbling, strengthens the circuit.
- **Overcorrecting into new distortions.** Without a clear replacement, some fall into trauma generalisations - blanket distrust of women, avoidance of intimacy, rigid control. These aren't new wires; they're survival loops dressed up as solutions.
- **Practising only in the storm.** Waiting for the hardest moments to test the new reflex sets you up for failure. It's in low-stakes practice - journalling, safe conversations, small boundaries - that the reflex is built strong enough to hold during crisis.
- **Seeking perfection instead of progress.** The new wiring doesn't need to be flawless to be effective. Even partial attempts - one sentence voiced, one feeling named, one pause taken - are victories.

The goal of Step 3 is not to become flawless in one leap. The goal is to make replacement a habit: every old wire you spot and crack open, you also pair with something new. These alternatives gather strength until they stop feeling like "alternatives" at all - they become your default wiring.

Step 4 - Repetition and Reinforcement

Rewiring doesn't happen in a single breakthrough. It happens in the quiet grind of practice. Insight sparks change, but repetition cements it. Every time you rehearse the healthier alternative, you are laying down fresh tracks in your nervous system. Every time you return to the new path instead of the old reflex, you strengthen the circuit you want to keep.

At first, the practice feels awkward. Your words come out shaky. Your pauses feel unnatural. The reflex still lurks, waiting for its chance to snap back into place. This is normal. The nervous system always prefers the well-worn track, because it costs less energy. But with each rehearsal, the balance shifts. The new path grows clearer, smoother, more automatic. What once felt forced becomes fluid. What once felt unsafe becomes second nature.

Repetition Teaches Safety

Your nervous system does not learn from ideas - it learns from outcomes. You can tell yourself a thousand times that you are safe to speak, safe to feel, safe to stay - but unless the body experiences it, the wiring won't update. The old reflex will still fire, because it has proof from years of survival experience. The only way to shift that balance is to provide new proof, moment by moment.

Every time you take a healthier action and nothing catastrophic happens, you are teaching your body a new lesson: safety is possible here.

- "I spoke a truth, and I wasn't punished."
- "I stayed present, and the world didn't collapse."
- "I expressed anger, and it didn't destroy the relationship."
- "I said no, and I wasn't abandoned."
- "I let go of control, and the world kept turning."

Each of these becomes a data point in the nervous system's ledger. The more data you accumulate, the harder it is for the old reflex to keep its grip. At first, the new entries are faint pencil marks compared to the bold ink of old experiences. But with every repetition, the lines darken. What once felt like an experiment becomes a pattern.

This is how repetition rewrites the body's memory. Survival taught you that speaking truth was dangerous, that staying present was

unbearable, that saying no would bring rejection. Each repetition offers counter-evidence. And slowly, your body begins to refile those memories - not under *danger* but under *possible*.

At some point, the shift becomes noticeable. The old reflex doesn't vanish, but it starts arriving later, weaker, less convincing. Instead of leaping in first, it lingers in the background while the new choice steps forward. That's when you know your nervous system has begun to treat the healthier wire as the default: the one it reaches for automatically, not the one it has to be talked into.

Repetition, then, is not just practice. It is persuasion. You are persuading your body that what was once unsafe can now be trusted. And like any persuasion, it doesn't work by argument alone. It works by proof, gathered again and again until the new story holds more weight than the old.

The Practice Of Reinforcement

Repetition alone is not enough. What matters is how you repeat. A single burst of effort can feel powerful in the moment, but without reinforcement, it fades like a spark in the dark. For a new wire to stabilise, it needs more than practice - it needs practice with qualities that make it reliable.

There are three of these qualities: consistency, variation, and compassion.

- **Consistency** Change is not built on heroic gestures. You do not need one perfect conversation or one flawless act of honesty to prove yourself healed. What your nervous system trusts most is rhythm. Small, steady actions - speaking one truth each day, staying present for one extra breath, naming one feeling instead of pushing it down - accumulate far more power than dramatic breakthroughs. Think of it like weight training. One enormous lift impresses the ego. A hundred smaller, regular lifts build the muscle. Consistency signals to your body that this new response

is not an accident, not a fluke, but a trustworthy option it can reach for again and again.
- **Variation** The nervous system also learns by context. If you only practise in one safe pocket - speaking honestly with a close friend, for example - the wire may strengthen there, but remain weak elsewhere. True reinforcement requires variety. Try the new wire in different environments: at work, at home, in public, in private. Each new context adds breadth to the wiring, showing your body that this choice is safe not just *somewhere*, but *anywhere*. Without variation, the new reflex remains compartmentalised, like a skill you can only access in one room. With variation, it becomes portable, a reflex you can carry into every situation.
- **Compassion** Reinforcement is not a straight line. The old wire will fire again. Sometimes it will fire first. This is not evidence of failure - it is evidence of history. Reflexes laid down under abuse were practised thousands of times under threat. It would be unrealistic to expect them to vanish after a handful of healthier trials. Compassion means recognising that relapse is part of learning. Each time you return to the healthier choice, even after the old reflex has flared, you are reinforcing it further. The return counts. The comeback is itself a form of practice. Compassion turns what could feel like failure into proof that you are still in the process of strengthening the new wire.

Together, these three qualities give reinforcement its staying power. Consistency creates rhythm. Variation creates universality. Compassion creates longevity. Without them, repetition risks becoming fragile, dependent on specific moods or situations. With them, repetition becomes reinforcement - not just a new behaviour tried once, but a new reflex installed, stabilised, and trusted.

The Feel Of Rewiring

Repetition rarely feels graceful at the start. In fact, it often feels like you're failing. The first attempts at a new wire are clumsy - you search for words that don't come, you notice your tone stumble, you replay

the moment afterwards and wonder if you got it wrong. That awkwardness is not a sign you're broken. It is a sign you are learning.

Think of it like physical rehab after an injury. The first time you move the joint, it feels stiff, weak, unnatural. Your body hasn't yet remembered how to move freely in this new way. But those shaky repetitions are exactly what wake the muscle up. In the same way, the emotional stumbles are proof you are in the training zone. They are the nervous system's version of micro-tears in the muscle - uncomfortable in the moment, but essential for growth.

At times, the old reflex will try to reassert itself. You'll feel the familiar urge to suppress, to smooth things over, to disconnect. The act of choosing differently may come out jagged, halting, or even a little louder than intended. That is normal. You are disrupting automatic wiring and laying down a new circuit. Like a toddler learning to walk, your steps will be unsteady before they become confident.

In time, the clumsiness shifts. The sentences flow more naturally. The pause before choosing presence grows shorter. The "healthy wire" no longer feels like an act you are forcing - it feels like an option that arrives on its own. This is the nervous system updating its map. Each awkward attempt becomes a deposit into that update, teaching your body and brain that the new path is not only survivable, but safe, and eventually effortless.

Clumsiness, then, is not failure. It is the sound of rewiring in motion.

Why Reinforcement Matters

Reinforcement is real reconditioning.

In Step 3 of the emotional processing cycle - **Memory Recall & Conditioning** - the nervous system looks back and asks, *"What happened last time I tried this?"* For survivors, those shelves are often filled with painful lessons: when you spoke up, you were punished; when you showed anger, you were shamed; when you reached for comfort, you were rejected. The body doesn't invent its reflexes - it remembers them.

Repetition is what replaces those records. Each time you choose a healthier move and survive it, a new memory is laid down. You spoke a truth and you weren't punished. You stayed present and nothing collapsed. You expressed anger and the relationship held. In time, these new memories begin to outweigh the old ones. The nervous system no longer automatically recalls threat - it starts to recall safety.

This is the essence of reinforcement: the steady practice of proving to yourself that the new path is survivable. Awareness spotted the faulty wire. Interrupts cracked it open. Installation supplied the new response. Reinforcement tells the body, *"This isn't just possible - it's safe."*

Step 5 – Integration And Expansion

Integration is the moment when the hard work of repair stops feeling like deliberate practice and begins to feel like part of who you are. Up until now, every stage has asked for effort - to notice the old reflex, to break its momentum, to choose an alternative, to repeat it until it sticks. Integration is when those actions shift from being something you *do* into something you *are*. The healthier wiring no longer has to be forced into place; it begins to run on its own, quietly guiding your choices and holding you steady in situations that once knocked you off balance.

But integration is not just about stabilising one repair. It is also about expansion. Once a single pathway proves it can hold, your awareness sharpens to the neighbouring wires still tangled in survival patterns. You begin to see how one reflex is tied to another - how silencing anger may connect to avoiding sadness, or how fawning in conflict may be linked to over-controlling in daily life. Each recognition is not a setback but an opening. The same cycle that rebuilt one circuit can now be applied again, widening the scope of repair and gradually restoring coherence across your emotional system.

This step matters because it marks the transition from survival work to embodied change. Without integration, recovery remains fragile - a handful of techniques you can manage when conditions are perfect.

With integration and expansion, those techniques transform into a lived foundation. Recovery ceases to be something you practise on the side; it becomes the way your nervous system moves through the world.

How It Shows Up (Experiential Markers)

Integration does not announce itself with fireworks or a single breakthrough moment. It reveals itself in subtle shifts - the kinds of ordinary experiences that suddenly feel lighter, steadier, and more natural than they once did. These are the signs that your nervous system has learned to hold the new wiring without collapse:

- **Conversations flow in real time.** Words come as you need them, without hours of mental rehearsal beforehand. You notice yourself responding in the moment rather than scripting every move.
- **Truth feels survivable.** You speak what matters - even when it carries risk - and instead of bracing for punishment or panic, your body holds steady.
- **Emotions complete their cycle.** A feeling rises, is expressed, makes sense, and then settles into storage - rather than being cut off halfway, suppressed, or spun endlessly in your mind.
- **The body softens**. Breath anchors lower in the belly. Shoulders unclench. The jaw eases. Even silence shifts - from a space that once felt dangerous to one you can rest inside.
- **Conflict no longer drains you.** Disagreements can happen and end without leaving you trembling or replaying them for hours. Your system begins to trust that repair is possible.

These markers are not dramatic, but they are profound. They are the quiet evidence that the nervous system is beginning to live by the new wire.

Holding The Cycle

Step 5 is the point where the emotional process can finally run its full course without collapsing. The natural current of feeling → expression → sense-making → storage holds together, uninterrupted by suppression, avoidance, or erasure. What once demanded vigilance - noticing, catching, correcting - now unfolds as a steady rhythm your body trusts. The circuit no longer needs to be forced. It runs clean on its own.

This is also the stage where expansion begins. A wire that has stabilised does not stand alone; it sits among others. And as one becomes clear, the surrounding patterns come into focus:

- The reflex that once silenced anger may reveal its neighbour - the wire that numbs sadness.
- The habit of fawning may show its link to the deeper pull of avoiding conflict altogether.
- The instinct to over-control may uncover the dissociative reflex hiding beneath it.

Integration does not close the work; it widens it. Each neighbouring wire you notice is not a setback, but an opening. It is an invitation to bring the same cycle - awareness, interruption, installation, reinforcement - to new ground. In this way, recovery does not stop at one repaired circuit. It expands outward, strengthening the emotional landscape until the system as a whole is rewired to hold steady.

Why It Matters

Integration and expansion mark the shift from survival tools to identity. Up until now, the work has been deliberate - noticing the reflex, interrupting it, choosing differently, rehearsing until it holds. Without integration, that wiring remains fragile, only reliable when the conditions are safe, predictable, and controlled. But once integration takes root, the nervous system itself takes over the job. What was once a technique becomes a reflex. What was once effort becomes ease.

Expansion ensures this change is not confined to one corner of life. As the healthier wiring proves itself in conversation, it extends into conflict. As it holds in private, it carries into public. Each new circuit reinforces the last, until the nervous system is not just patching old breaks but building a stronger whole.

This is not recovery techniques in motion – it is reconditioning. It is the point where the body no longer rehearses survival, but embodies safety.

Conclusion

The goal of this work is to restore something essential that abuse tried to take away — your natural, healthy connection to your feelings.

For too long, emotions may have felt unsafe, distorted, or hijacked. You may have braced against them, doubted them, or been told they weren't valid. But emotions are not the enemy. They are signals, guides, and anchors - meant to move through you, not trap you.

By walking through these steps - awareness, interruption, replacement, reinforcement, and integration - you are showing your nervous system that feelings can be trusted again. Anger can protect without destroying. Sadness can move without swallowing you. Joy can arrive without guilt. Presence can hold without fear.

Reconnecting with your feelings means reclaiming your compass. It means living in a way where your emotions no longer run you into survival loops, but instead carry you into clarity, connection, and choice.

This is not a quick fix. But every cycle you run cleanly is proof of change. Every time you let a feeling rise, move, and settle without hijack, you are laying down new wiring. Slowly, steadily, this becomes not just something you practise, but who you are.

You've already taken the hardest step by opening this book. Keep going. Keep trusting your feelings. They are not broken - they are waiting to bring you home to yourself.

If you need help spotting the loops, holding steady through the rewiring, or simply having a safe place to practise new responses – we're here.

No matter how many times you have been knocked down, you can Stand Again.

Glossary

Abuser-Driven Hijacks
Tactics an abuser uses to deliberately interfere with your emotional process. Examples include gaslighting, flooding, or conditioning you to respond in specific ways.

Awareness
The first step of the healthy emotional cycle — noticing when something sparks a feeling in you.

Balloon Effect

The build-up of suppressed emotions over time. Each time a feeling is pushed down, it adds pressure — like air forced into a balloon. The emotion doesn't disappear; it compresses. Eventually the balloon leaks (background anxiety, irritability), bursts suddenly (explosive reaction), or releases in the wrong direction (misdirected at someone who wasn't the cause).

Conditioning
When repeated experiences (positive or negative) teach your nervous system to react in a certain way. In abuse, conditioning often teaches you to shut down or mistrust your feelings.

Crisis Shelving

A survival adaptation where an emotion is felt but deliberately set aside before sense-making can occur. The intention is to return to it later, but in abuse, "later" rarely comes. Shelved emotions accumulate unresolved, often surfacing later as disproportionate reactions or generalised heaviness.

Cue → Response Conditioning
A form of training where a neutral signal (like a slammed door or a sigh) becomes linked with a big emotional reaction (fear, panic, appeasement) — even if no threat follows.

Stand Again
Support for male victims of family violence

Dissociation
A survival response where you "check out" mentally or emotionally. You might feel numb, foggy, or as though you're watching life from the outside.

Emotional Cycle (Emotional Processing Cycle)
The natural sequence of feeling → expression → sense-making → learning → storage. Abuse interrupts or rewires this cycle, leaving emotions incomplete or distorted.

Emotional Dysregulation
When your emotions feel too big, too small, or out of proportion to the situation. You may explode over something minor, or feel flat when you expected to care.

Emotional Suppression
Shutting down or hiding emotions before they can be expressed. This is often learned in abuse as a way to stay safe.

Fawning
A survival response where you appease or over-please someone to reduce conflict. It can protect you in abuse, but often erases your own needs and voice.

Flooding
An abuser tactic where they overwhelm you with too much input — accusations, insults, or demands — so you can't process clearly and end up shutting down.

Gaslighting
A manipulation tactic where someone denies, distorts, or rewrites your reality, making you doubt your own memory, perception, or feelings.

Integration
The stage in recovery where new, healthier emotional responses stop feeling like effort and begin to run on their own as part of who you are.

Micro-Interrupt
A very small, deliberate action you use to interrupt an old survival

reflex — like taking one slow breath before answering, or relaxing your shoulders when they tense.

Mood Lability
Unstable emotional swings between extremes — for example, calm one moment, in tears the next, then suddenly flat and detached.

Protective Interrupts
Survival moves you make to shut down your own emotional cycle when it feels unsafe to continue (e.g., suppression, dissociation, fawning).

Reinforcement
Practising healthier emotional responses often enough that your nervous system starts to trust them as safe and automatic.

Schema Therapy
A therapeutic approach that identifies long-standing survival beliefs ("schemas") and helps replace them with healthier ones.

Sense-Making

The stage in the emotional processing cycle (Step 5) where you name and understand what you're feeling. It's the shift from raw sensation to recognised emotion — from "something is happening in my body" to "I feel angry" or "I feel sad." In abuse, this step is often hijacked, skipped, or rewritten by the abuser.

Somatic Experiencing
A body-based therapy that helps you notice and tolerate physical sensations linked to emotions, so you can process them without shutting down.

Trauma Conditioning
The way abuse shapes your nervous system over time, training you to expect danger, suppress emotions, or run survival scripts.

Window of Tolerance
The emotional "zone" where you can stay present without being overwhelmed or shutting down. Abuse often shrinks or warps this window.

Stand Again
Support for male victims
of family violence

www.ingramcontent.com/pod-product-compliance
Lightning Source LLC
Chambersburg PA
CBHW042038100526
44587CB00030B/4481